The Craft of House-Brewing

by

Clive La Pensée

How to plant and maintain a hop-garden.
Making malt and mashing.
Matching beer to your water supply.
Setting up your own house- or micro-brewery.
How to build an outhouse brewing machine.

Montag Publications

Published by Montag Publications.
6, Minster Avenue, Beverley, HU17 0NL, UK

Artwork and design by Annemarie.

Layout by Peter Bernard Shally & Stephen Richardson.
Printed by V. Richardson & Sons Ltd., Brekkes Building,
William Wright Dock, Hull, HU1 2ET, UK

ISBN 0 9515685 6 6

Contents

List of Illustrations

Charts

Graphs

BRAXONIA™

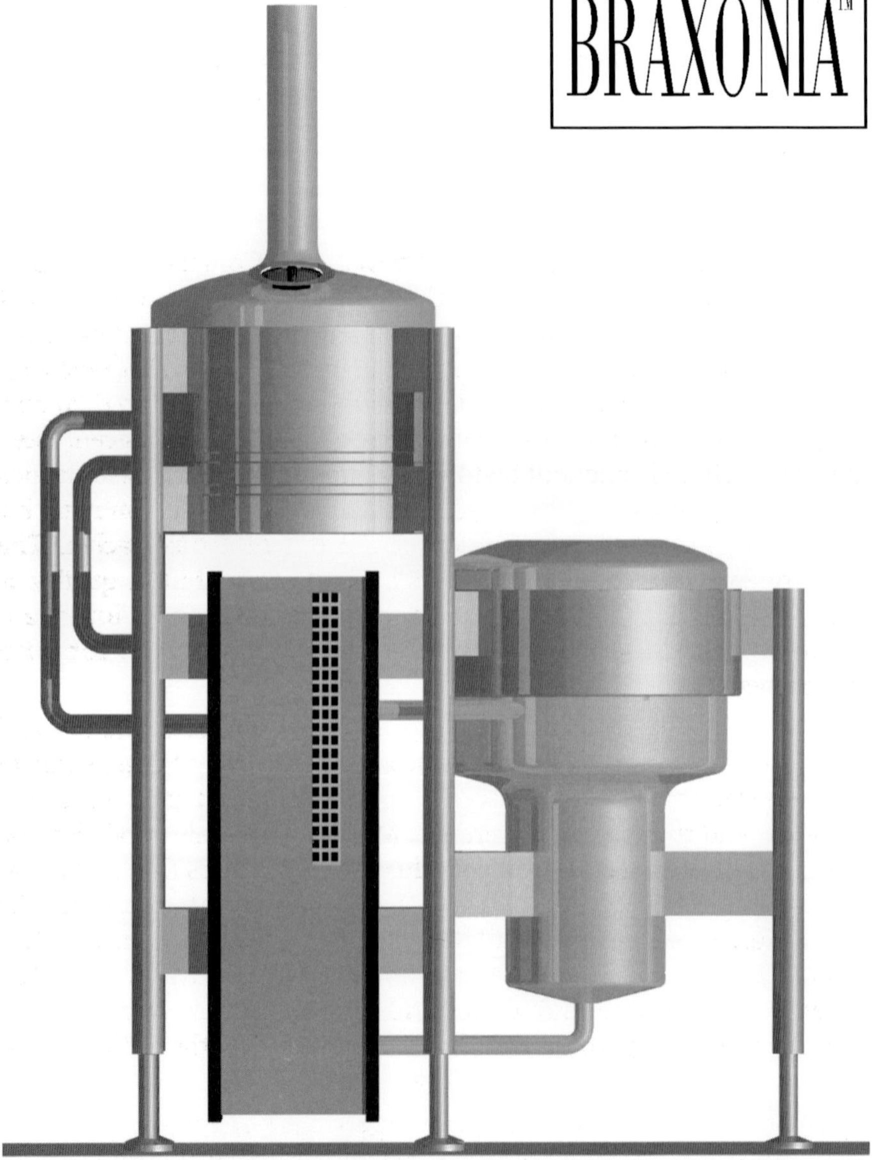

House-Brewing into the 21st century. A computer controlled, twenty litre full brewing system.

The Craft of House-Brewing.

One bushel of malt absorbs 5 gallons of water. Notch your broomstick!
(Domestic Brewing. A Handbook for Families. 1843)

Introduction.

Six years have now passed since The Historical Companion to House-Brewing appeared, and it was the first book to go onto the UK Homebrew market in fifteen years. Imagine our consternation when it appeared almost to the day with Graham Wheeler's *Home Brewing*. Both books were revolutionary in their thinking. Both picked up on a long historical tradition that said, "if you want to brew decent beer, do it yourself". Throughout history, self interest and greed have steeped beer making in the sin and error of thinking it can be done quickly and easily, like shaking a Dundee Cake out of a mix packet. The consequence of this philosophy has been a steady shift in quality as kits became ever more popular. The mashers became an important minority in British Homebrew but they were catered for with disinterest.

"You can't live off the mashing market," the can makers and Homebrew retailers told me. Doubtless they are right. Neither Graham or I can claim to be living off books on mashing, but then we do not have to. And there is the difference. Making genuinely good ales and beers has always been a cottage industry and perhaps that is the way it has to be. Any attempt to pervert that uncomfortable truth results in a different product that will dissatisfy the purist drinker. That had been the premise of the first book and that was why I had relied so heavily on historical sources to write it. If you want to resurrect a cottage industry, perhaps you have to go back to the skills of that time.

The results of our labours were staggering! I'm not going to claim that it was all our doing, but the fact remains that within eighteen months of the *Companion* and Graham's book appearing, the can makers suddenly started promoting traditional beers such as porters, stouts, wheat beers etc. Retailers told me sales of malt, and some quite esoteric malts at that, were improving. They are still reluctant to switch the selling emphasis from kits to mashing ingredients and with few notable exceptions, will never encourage a kit man to mash. In the meantime the beer-kit end of the market also finds itself in crisis, mainly I believe because the manufacturers tried to be too user friendly and convince the beer lover that anyone can brew from a can. This is unfortunately not true. Many astute brewers brew very nicely thank you from a can, but they accept that a can of wort concentrate needs the same tender loving care as a mash. Part of the reason for the crisis has to be because many retailers find it difficult to give sound advice on brewing with kits or relate the advantages of mashing. Their problem is understandable. How do you impart the necessary knowledge to a beginner without making it sound as though he needs a diploma in brewing technology? Where should new brewers gain their expertise from? Most books on the market concentrate on imitating popular pub beers but the problem is these beers never taste like the pub beers they try to imitate (whatever they taste like), for the uncomfortable truth is that getting two beers to taste identical, even with the sophisticated control technology of a modern brewery, is very difficult and certainly impossible in the kitchen at home. We can't control the parameters such as temperature, malt characteristics, water quality, yeast and of course attenuation. During storage beer is a constantly changing biochemical power house. That is also why beer should taste different every day for the yeast and enzymes do not stop working just because we think the beer is ready to drink. It is a dynamically different drink by the hour. Why else did the old cellar master spend so much of his day in his beer cellar deciding, which barrel would be ready and when?

But that is all very inconvenient! Everyone wants a standard article that will have a guaranteed taste. Or at least that is what we are told we want. So the breweries use all sorts of smart chemical tricks to speed up the natural processes and then stop them in their tracks at just the right moment.

They too have a problem. Beer is normally only at its best for about six weeks. How are they to know how long a can will rest on a supermarket shelf or in our cupboards at home? My father served me a John Smiths' bitter a year past its drink-by date, and it still tasted exactly as the brewery had intended. I can't achieve this! When my beer is ready, it has to be drunk. On the other hand I do achieve far more interesting beers than commercial breweries even though not all of these flavours would win prizes!

So why do I keep advocating brewing your own when I admit it is such a minefield? Here are a few thoughts.

- You can control the quality and type of ingredient used.
- There are few limits to the variety of beers that can be brewed.
- You can control the brewing process and avoid the quick fix solutions that breweries nowadays resort to.
- Most important of course, it is such good fun to brew your own.

And so I think it is high time to fill in my readers with an update on ideas, some recipes they will never have heard of, and assault their good taste with a few they will wish I'd left buried beneath the dust of centuries. But my purpose is to show that many ideas that we treat with arrogance as well as a few that we use without knowing why, all have an excellent pedigree in history, sometimes thousands of years old.

This book is not for the faint hearted, nor for the beginner, but for house-brewers who enjoy a run for their money, who want to successfully have their own hop garden, and make their own malt or produce their own yeast strain. It is to them this book is dedicated and to whom I say, "notch your broomstick!"

A fourteenth century brewer, probably a monk, with his stick notched, stirring his mash in an early brewing machine.

Chapter one.

I want to be as smart as an Egyptian.

"History is bunk!" said that famous American Henry Ford. Of course car makers believe they must always look forward but we're not in the car business and I want to ask the questions, "Is there merit in looking even further back than even I normally do? Has the historical shift in the late industrial 20th century been to our advantage as consumers of food and drink or have we, like Ford, simply slimmed ourselves down to fit onto conveyor belt production"?

The fact remains that there is nothing worth having that someone hasn't already thought of. We may be able to improve on things, but as they say in Hollywood, "there are no new plots". Under these circumstances, let's investigate the biochemistry of the process we want to carry out by going right back to the beginning; to a time when people knew exactly where everything came from. And then we'll look at what we can learn and copy from eighteenth, nineteenth and early twentieth century brewers. These were times when brewers still had an intimate relationship with the things they used. I believe that we can only begin to truly enjoy our lives and the things we do, the hobbies we pursue, when we have re-established our relationship to the things we use. What better way to do it than brewing a decent pint?

So here is a chapter to humble you - it has all been done before - and encourage you - our hobby is part of the oldest of all creative human occupations.

Let's first look at what the conveyor belt has looked like for the last 150 years.

The five steps

1) The barley is steeped for 72 hours at around 8°C (46°F) during which time it swells and takes up water under huge osmotic pressure.
2) This barley is germinated during which time enzymes are produced which are able to break down starch into maltose. Maltose is the fuel the barley would use if allowed to grow.

3) The barley is dried to prevent the corn using valuable starch. The enzymes are dormant. The malt may be kilned to give it extra colour.
4) The malt is infused (mashed) with water at around 65°C (149°F) and the enzymes resume their work of breaking starch up into maltose units.
5) The water soluble material, including maltose, is washed from the husks, flavoured and fermented.

Amazingly, these same five steps can be found throughout history and are in fact our definition of beer.

The advantage of looking back at the variety of methods utilised to achieve these five steps reveals not the dozen or so beers we can easily acquire in a bar or supermarket, but a vast spectrum of flavours and nuances that only the house-brewer can hope to recreate. My favourite beer pastime at present is to try to get back to the very beginning.

If only I could be as smart as an Egyptian.

There is little doubt that the Egyptians along with the Babylonians were the first brewers and it is quite remarkable how little the brewing process has changed in the ensuing ten thousand years. Of course there are differences between then and now, but amazingly these differences seem to be limited to the herbs and spices used to flavour the beer as well as the technology involved, rather than in the brewing biochemistry. And isn't it nice to know that our hobby has a ten thousand year tradition. It is because I'm working in such a long tradition while home-brewers with their cans of concentrate only go back about 30 years, that I make the distinction between House-Brewing:- that which has been practised domestically for so long, and home brewing. The latter has been virtually reduced to the lowest common denominator within decades of its re-emergence as a domestic activity.

I must confess to having always dreamt of brewing a beer from a recipe nearly as old as history itself and because the Egyptians couldn't resist writing everything down they did, it is quite likely that we can

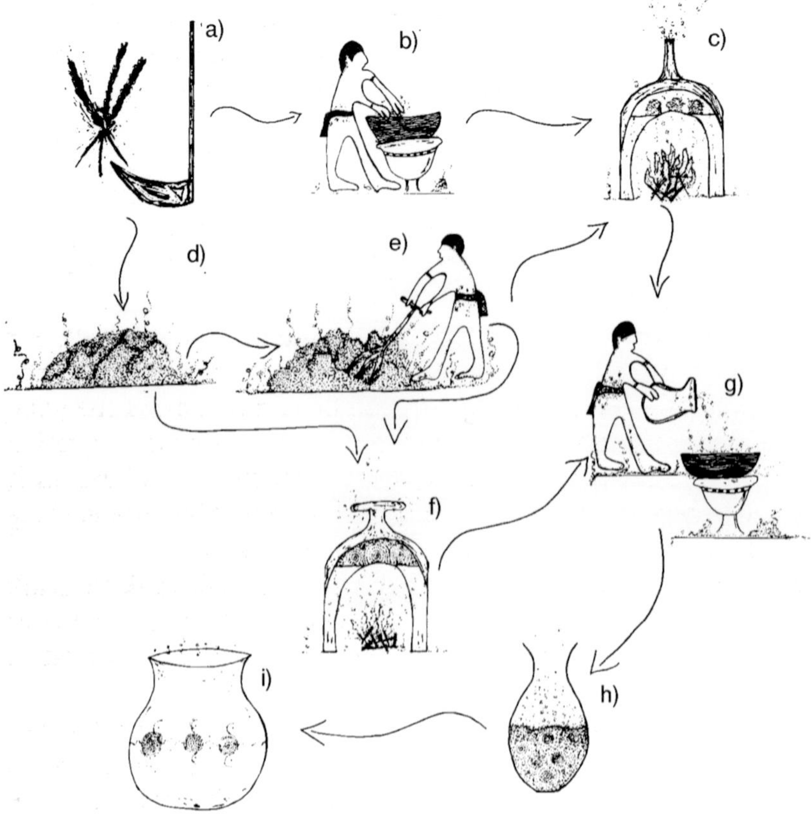

Flow chart of Ancient malting and brewing.

Brewing with beer loaves.
The barley and spelt were often harvested still green (a). In Egypt such grains were used for making beer loaves (b), which were gently baked (c) to form malt which would also start to ferment. Soluble material was washed from the loaves (g) or the loaves broken into pieces to ferment (h) to make drinks such as Fokka (i).

Brewing with malt.
Sometimes the grain was germinated in a cool place such as an underground hole and then wetted and dried and turned until it broke up. This was included in the loaves (d-e-c).
Green malt or wet harvested grain was dried in ovens prior to use (d-f) and then mashed (g).
The exact method used depended on regional preferences.

brew something today fairly close to what they drank all those thousands of years ago. A visit to a museum with a good Department of Egyptian Studies reveals that the coffins of any person possessing special skills, had details of those skills written on the inside of their coffin so that the deceased would have a good start in his afterlife. Important papyrus and other artifacts were also buried along with them giving details of the life they had led and of common day occurrences at that time. As brewing was big business in Ancient Egypt there are plenty of sources to work from.

Thus it is we know that the Egyptians were prolific drinkers. For example there were periods in their history when one day of the calender was set aside for drunkenness. The completion of the wine harvest and the making of the new vintage inaugurated the Egyptian New Year. Wine though was not as widely consumed as beer, as it mainly had to be imported, for it is a general rule that barley and vines do not appreciate the same climatic and soil conditions.

It was considered quite proper for women of high rank to drink themselves to nausea and senselessness and for the wine and beer servers, who were also frequently women, to encourage immodest drinking.

Such bouts were accompanied by licentious behaviour of both sexes, and the girls and women who brewed beer, served it, and provided entertainment in the taverns as singers, were also prostitutes. There is little doubt that an accepted part of the functions of taverns was also as brothels.

"Do not have intercourse with a zither player so that thou art not caught in her snares," wrote one ancient scribe.

The amounts that were brewed for a feast must have placed considerable strain on their economy for despite their undoubted agricultural skills a good harvest was a very fickle thing, and they must have devoted a considerable amount of their grain production to making beer. Consider that according to Herodotus every soldier was allowed to drink enough wine to become drunk and anointed with oil each day as on a holiday in Egypt. The Royal Bodyguard consisted of two thousand men and each received four measures of wine. A mother who brought her son to school would carry for him three loaves of bread and two jars of beer daily.

We may think that the beer was probably thin and low in alcohol as was probably the case in *David Copperfield* when the boys were served so-called table beer for breakfast. Not so in Egypt one believes!! Of course we have no information on the alcoholic strength of their beer and it was certainly brewed for nutrition as well as alcohol, but the descriptions of the ill effects of beer drinking are thought to indicate that it may have been very powerful stuff in one way or another. After all many modern beer drinkers would find it quite impossible to get very drunk on beer, because we find it difficult to cope with the volume that would be needed to get us drunk at say 5% alcohol by volume. Historians believe the ancient Egyptians seem not to have suffered any limitations to their state of inebriation due to volume, but I'll return to problems of alcohol percent. I think our interpretation of their drinking bouts may be at variance with what they actually drank and why they drank it.

Yoghurt beers.

Beer and bread were always intimately linked in antique society. One may rightly assume that the obvious connection was the use of grain and yeast in both processes, but I think it goes a bit deeper than that. We know the Egyptians had several methods of extracting the sugar from the grain. Often the grain was moistened and left in a container buried in the ground until germination started. Then the green malt was ground, made into loaves with some sour dough or leaven and baked just long enough for a crust to form. The inside remained warm but not cooked.

"The loaves were stored until beer was required," is the historian's statement which shows that the historians don't appreciate the biochemistry of the process as well as the Egyptians did. The loaves were stored I believe until it was judged that the enzymes produced in the green malt and released during the pot buried in the ground phase, had broken down the heavy starch molecules to produce fermentable maltose. This would immediately be tackled by the leaven and converted to alcohol among other things. The crust trapped the whole process in its own microcosm, which we today call a mash tun or bucket. Incidently, I believe that very little yeast (a fungus) fermentation took place but rather a so-called sour dough fermentation, which uses a bacterium, *lactobacillus plantarum,* which undoubtedly gave the beer a very sour flavour. It would also account for the copious reports that beer gave the drinker a very poorly tummy due to the acidity. This acid beer is still brewed by the Fellah of Egypt and known as *BOOZAH*. Steady!!! The Oxford Dictionary gives the Low German word Buizen as the correct etymology for booze. Shame!

Now I said that we believe the Egyptian beer must have been strong. Maybe the ill effects of drinking were down to the sour dough fermentation and because relatively little alcoholic fermentation took place I suggest they had to drink large quantities in order to reach inebriation! Throwing up became a necessary evil. It certainly showed dedication to the task if they regularly faced 5 pints of yoghurt.

And one may not forget the medicinal need to vomit. Egyptian medicine saw vomiting as a desirable purging of the system. The sour beer may have been drunk in such huge quantities in the belief that vomiting was doing good and hence the serving girls were fulfilling the role of the well-meaning nanny, encouraging her charges to take their medicine. Perhaps the drunkenness and licentious behaviour were readily accepted by-products of the treatment. Certainly, the addition of medicinal herbs to beer was the common way of administering them.

The medicinal use of beer in ancient times, was also to induce vomiting.

Ancient civilizations also knew how to make malt as we understand it and in a way we would instantly recognise. If the Egyptians possessed such knowledge, why make loaves first? X-ray pictures of Egyptian Mummies show that by their mid-teens, many Egyptians suffered from a condition called attrition.

This is caused by grit or sand in the flour, which wears away the teeth quicker than the body can regenerate them. Very painful. I suggest that by mashing and fermenting the grain inside the loaf and then running water over the pulp to extract the soluble alcohol and other corn substance, it was relatively easy to remove the grit, which would either hang onto the insoluble corn substance or if it were washed through, would settle out as sediment, allowing the beer to be decanted off. Perhaps grains from harvests that contained a lot of grit were set aside for beer making.

Green harvests.

Malt was also produced for beer in Britain before the Roman invasion although its manufacture may not have been entirely intentional. It does give us an idea of how beer could have been invented in ancient society.

Some communities were still nomadic, following food and water, while others lived in fixed places, moving only when conditions of pestilence or war forced them to. As beer was invented independently in innumerable places on the globe, the type of society does not seem to have been that germane to its discovery. Whether the population were still wanderers or had become sedentary, I'm sure there was pressure to harvest when it was safe or convenient rather than when the corn was actually ripe and dry. It was common practice to harvest the grain while still green if that were advantageous. A bird in the hand has always been worth two in a bush. In England at the time of the Roman invasion (55 BC) the green grain was then kilned in T or Y shaped clay ovens to dry it for storing. If this drying were not thorough or the grain was stored damp, the enzyme factory started up again and maltose was made from the starch. A gruel made from such grain tasted sweet and if it were left open for any length of time then wild yeasts settled, fermentation set in and beer produced. A few sprigs of bog myrtle from the local swamp and you couldn't tell it from a Budweiser (maybe). Yes, even the bland tastes of the modern pale lager market have a pedigree in history, for it was common right through to the Renaissance not to flavour beer at all. They certainly did not always have the quite typical flavour, which we recognise today in a good craft brewed beer.

Ancient beers.

I'd love to be able to tell you how to brew and serve some Egyptian beer, one third safflower seed, or an Ancient Briton beer, made only of green malt and tansy but my research has only got me as far as asking HOW. Now that I'm some way to answering that question I can move on to the doing phase. To this end I've dug a pond in my garden and about one quarter of it is set aside as a wet area. Bog myrtle has been planted but is still too small to even allow a sampler. Bog myrtle is a crucial plant as it was the main forerunner of hops and held a virtual monopoly in beer flavouring up until the 16th century. Next year... Who knows? We may once again know how Ale really tasted for Ale was once the name given to the grut beers flavoured with plants such as myrtle. Beer became the name reserved for the new-fangled hop beers.

Although I grow my own hops and our house beer is exclusively flavoured with hops, it is a fascinating exercise to investigate the other flavours possible. To that end I have planted tansy, woodruff, wormwood, mugwort, lemon balm, sage and pennyroyal. My alehoof, horehound and hyssop have died but comfrey, dandelion and nettle are simply indestructible. Bittering agents such as tansy or bog myrtle are known as hop surrogates as they render a similar flavour to that of hops (cf. surrogates). Lemon balm on the other hand produces a beer of quite different qualities. What did the Egyptians use? Unfortunately in my cool North European garden with average summer temperatures around 16°C, I'm unlikely to be able to flavour with any variety of substances. I can get hold of safflower seeds and dried dates but essentially the practical research will have to be done by some enthusiastic California brewer who does not mind trying to recreate a miniature Garden of Babylon out there in the yard. I shall keep working on Bog Myrtle Ales, but here are some thoughts on how I would brew Egyptian beer if I had the weather to do it.

Egyptian Beer.

Before we can start brewing we must look at the Egyptian preference for spicing their beer and what type of grain they used. Barley was treated by a process, which we would recognise as malting but it seems certain that they did not use the modern two row variety but the six row, which was also known and still used by the Celts in the 6th century AD. The term two row or six row refers to the number of rows of seeds to be found on the ear. Six row varieties don't have much of a following any more, but were still used until the late fifties, although they contain much less corn substance per grain even if more grains were produced. Various types of barley were used in antiquity in the near and middle east as well as spelt.

Humulus lupulus was not to become a recognized flavouring for beer until the 9th century in Germany and the 15th century elsewhere but the lupin *lupinus termis* and skirret, a type of radish, were used according to Lutz. How they were added to the beer is not at all clear but as there is no record of beer having been boiled it is safe to assume that they were added at the end of the production stage and left to infuse. Here is a recipe rendered usable for us by Lutz. Let us name it after its ancient Egyptian brewer of the town of Panopolis. The first step is to make the loaves.

The Grain was often worked into loaves before gentle baking to make malt.

Making beer loaves for Zosimus Beer.

First make some leaven as a rising agent for the loaves. Leaven can be made by mixing flour (nowadays usually rye flour) with water and standing it in a covered bowl for a few days. (*Historical Companion to House-Brewing page 49*)

1. Steep 2.2 kg (5 lbs) best barley for 1 day and drain it and lay it overnight (in the dark) in a draught free place.
2. Steep it again for another 6 hours.
3. Pour the grain into the bucket with the perforated base and wet and dry the grain until it becomes shredded.
4. Shake it and rub it in the sunlight until it falls apart for the must is bitter.

Ed Hitchcock reports in detail his attempt to follow this process. He put the grain into 1 litre jars with perforated lids and drained and soaked the grain at 12 hour intervals until signs of germination were evident. He records the grain then having a vinegary smell. I think that with hindsight his perforations did not allow enough air in.

His green malt also produced a white thick starchy paste. Again I have to suspect suffocation of the grain. I have found that green barley and wheat malt both squash when put through a grinder but remain essentially friable and powdery.

I also wondered if the grain used in Babylonia for this part of the process was actually germinated or simply worked with water until it was easy to squash. Sounds like something Ed and I will have to put our heads together on, for the historical interpretations of Lutz and Huber seem to offer both variations.

Here we have a departure from modern technique. Modern maltsters always germinate in the dark or in blue light to prevent inevitable greening through photosynthesis. The chlorophyll produced during photosynthesis is reputed to give the malt a bitter flavour.

5. Grind the damp malt, add leaven and form it into loaves.

6a. Either bake the loaves gently and whenever the loaves rise place them in a sieve and run a very gentle stream of water over them to dissolve up the sweetness. Catch this water in a pail and allow it to ferment.

or 6b. Others broke the loaves up once they started to rise and cast the pieces into a vat with water. This was heated so gently that there was no danger of any frothing nor even of exceeding body heat and kept warm until there was no further sign of fermentation.

Ed opted for baking flat biscuits without any leaven. He was interpreting a recipe gleaned from an ancient Summarian Hymn unknown to me but I think that high loaves partially baked, leaving the insides damp and able to mash and maybe even ferment, makes more sense. The addition of leaven is recorded by Lutz. He suggests grinding the green malt, making it into loaves with the addition of leaven and cooking it raw. Whenever the loaves start to rise the sweetened water is run off from the loaf using a strainer or sieve. Others lightly baked the loaves and then broke them into pieces and mashed by treading with the feet.

Here is a problem of interpretation that is not easy to solve. It all hangs from the question, "Why make loaves in the first place?" Ed and his co-workers see the loaves as a malt surrogate. In fact the loaves are just another way of making and storing malt. This argument is strong for there is little doubt that the loaves were sometimes baked gently to yield pale beer and sometimes baked more strongly for colour, much the same way as we finish malt nowadays for different beers.

As I've already stated, I interpret the loaf making as being an integral part of the brewing process, a kind of encapsulated mash. Why else would leaven be added to the loaves? The most obvious solution to this argument is that both systems were practised in various parts of the Near and Middle East. In Mesopotamia the loaves were a malting process and in Egypt they belonged to the brewer.

7. When the beer loaves had been thoroughly kneaded and stirred the solids were strained from the liquid, (sometimes pressed out using specially made bowls with a hole in the base for the purpose) and the liquid filled into earthenware jugs.

   We may use bottles.

8. The beer was drunk as soon as it was needed and flavoured by hanging whatever herb or spice was to be used into the jug of beer for several minutes before consumption. It may also have been added to the beer as it was bottled. Certain flavours, (e.g. saffron seeds) were added to the grain as the loaves were being made.

Making Green Malt (Germinated Barley).

Some recipes required the grain to be germinated, although it may not have been dried. Presumably then the ancient Egyptians used the green malt immediately and must have understood that the germinated barley provided them with a sweeter wort than the loaves on their own.

Green malt was prepared by digging a hole and placing a pot with wet barley in it until it was germinated. The hole served no other purpose but to keep the temperature down, so the antique brewers already understood the need for the low germination temperatures, which the modern maltster uses. I don't dig holes in the garden but help myself better by using a fridge or a cool shed. Use the description of green malt preparation given later in this volume, but leave out the drying stage to make Egyptian malt.

An alternative method of making oriental beer has been interpreted by Ludwig Borchardt who did much of the major interpretational work on the hieroglyphics without considering the practical implications of the method he handed down to us. He was after all a historian, not a brewer. Here is my interpretation of his method.

Borchardt's Babylonian Black Beer.

Ingredients.

Make a beer loaf as described above in the Zosimus Beer. Use about 1.2 kg ($2^1/_2$ lbs) of grain. As this is a black beer it would seem that the loaves were more strongly baked than usual to render the beer some colour.

Make 1.8 kg (3.6 lbs) germinated barley as described above.

900g spelt. (Use wheat. Spelt is an early form of wheat, which we are not likely to find any more, unless travelling in the Middle East).

The cheapest black beer used only barley but the more up-market the recipes, the more spelt was added. We are at a loss as to the flavouring but dried dates were very common in Babylonia as a beverage flavouring and if these were added to the wort prior to fermentation, then the wild yeasts, which they naturally carry, surely gave the fermentation a flying start and removed the need for leaven, which would have made the beer sour. Many texts suggest the Babylonians flavoured with honey but this is uncertain for it may not be bee-honey that is meant but a thickened mixture of various fruit juices. Suddenly the North European habit of flavouring beer with strawberries, cherries or pineapple, seems to have good pedigree.

Many historians question the need for the ancient brewers to have made malt. Lutz in fact considers the translation of malt to be an error, for malt would seem to be out of place in the Babylonian method. He supposes that to make green malt, a hole was dug in the ground and the barley simply poured in and covered and left until it showed signs of germination and reports that at the time of his studies (1920s) this method was still in use in Egypt. Of course the use of malt brings the pH of the mash right down into the acidic range, which probably inhibits some of the more unpleasant and maybe dangerous products of aerobic sour mashes. The lactobacillus is ever present on the grain husks don't forget. Whether the germination in itself produces enough

Beer was drunk very young through straws from the centre of the vessel, to avoid the lumps that hadn't settled out.

acid buffer is questionable. Remember, modern brewers can regulate mash pH using dark heavily roasted malts. I don't find it hard to believe that the ancient brewers were smart enough to have discovered the advantages of drying the green malt made by the hole in the ground method. Surely during the thousands of years that these amazing people were making beer, someone must have got their timing wrong, had the green malt ready too early and left it laying in the hot African sun until the time was more precipitous and inadvertently made some malt!

Emmerbier.

One of the most interesting and most written and researched beers of the ancient orient is Spelt-beer. Much of the original work on this topic was done by E. Huber who researched this beer ninety years ago. He called it Emmerbier, Emmer being German for a rough winter wheat with a particularly firm husk, which needs special treatment during threshing to remove it. This makes it a suitable choice for malting as one of the major problems with wheat is the lack of protective husk during germination.

Emmerbier was probably rarely made only with wheat. Barley was a frequent adjunct, each addition of barley producing a different quality of beer.

The particular oddity about Emmerbier is that it was often made to be very sweet and viscous, rather like malt extract. Here are a few variations as interpreted by Huber.

Black Emmerbier.

Use the Babylonian method to mash:

1. Remove all husks using a pestle and mortar or some other mill.
2. Dampen the grain and allow it to germinate.
3. Squash the green barley malt and spelt in a wide mill and form the barley grain pulp into loaves. There is no indication that spelt was altered.
4. Bake the loaves gently to form malt. For a dark beer bake the loaves more strongly.

5. Break the cold loaves into pieces and put them into a mash tun with the squashed wet spelt and some cinnamon to taste and other aromatic plants available. Add enough water to provide for a thin mash.
6. Bring the mash slowly to the boil over 2 hours. (This is guess work but one believes the volume of the mash was reduced by some 25% during the boiling phase. The mash should be quite syrupy).
7. Pour the mash through a coarse sieve, probably some woven grass that we would find similar to coconut matting.
8. Seal the syrup in a jar or glass until shortly before it is needed, then dilute it with water to give a gravity of 1.040 and ferment with a top fermenting yeast. (Maybe add some dried dates and allow the wild yeasts to work on the wort.)
9. Serve as soon as the beer has fermented out.
10. Drink the beer through long straws that stretch deep into the centre of the pot containing the beer. This technique eliminates floaters and sediment.

Here are some of the variations on Summarian Emmerbier. All quantities are given in litres and are the amounts delivered to a brewer for the purpose of making the malt or loaves. The husk-free spelt was used untreated. As a rule of thumb the volume of corn used usually approximates to the volume of beer brewed. The red beer must have been a double or treble beer of around 10-12%.

Beer name	Spelt	Barley malt	Pale loaves	Dark loaves	Volume brewed
Black beer	0.25	9	4.5	9	20
Summarian Kulbacher	9	9	3	0	20
Red beer	25	25	20	0	20
Prima beer	9	15	15	0	50
Table beer	0	20	0	0	20

Chapter two.

The Water We Use.

The proper season for brewing is between October and March but reigning opinion is not reliable for the former is too warm and the latter too close to spring. The water may in October still have the smell of the weeds that have grown in it. Some waters likewise breed innumerable quantities of insects and this is said to cause a very strong fermentation.

Poole 1783

Water.

And we think we have problems with unreliable water supplies. Our problems nowadays have quite different causes but if we can demonstrate that the problems and observations of yesteryear have plausible scientific explanations, we will have more confidence in the skill and wisdom of historical brewers, for it is their methods that offer themselves most readily to us in the kitchens of today. It is therefore valuable and interesting to ask why innumerable quantities of insects should cause an over-vigorous fermentation? Does this observation from over 200 years ago have a scientific explanation? In 1783 concepts such as pH and mineral fertilizers were not on the tips of anyone's tongue, so we may assume that the relationship between high insect concentrations and fast fermentations was an empirical observation (i.e. formed without theoretical knowledge).

Nowadays one can buy pH papers and nitrate determining sticks from an aquarium shop and any experienced fish keeper knows that the waste products from animals and decomposing organic material in a tank lead to high nitrogen and phosphorous concentrations being present as phosphate, ammonium and nitrate ions. What do we use as yeast nutrient, available in little packets from the Homebrew shop? Following are some typical yeast nutrient values.

Chemical Compound	% by weight	Desirable constituent
Ammonium phosphate	73	nitrogen/phosphorous
Potassium phosphate	12	potassium/phosphorous
Potassium chloride	5	potassium chloride
Magnesium sulphate	2.5	magnesium
Calcium phosphate	2.5	calcium/phosphorous
Aneurine hydrochloride	5	vitamin B

Ions and Chlorine.

Ammonium ions and phosphate ions are the main constituents, and although nitrates present in water of high organic content are reputed to be detrimental to yeast, presumably their effect is outweighed by the presence of ammonium and phosphate ions. Viewed in this light it is hardly surprising that water that is high in organic material causes a rash fermentation.

What early brewers didn't have to contend with are the far more detrimental chlorine levels in our modern water supply. These are supposed to affect healthy fermentation and can't be good for the mash either but I'm not convinced that this is such a problem that we should spend large sums of money on water filters or treatment plants. After all, chlorine is not very soluble in water and consequently fairly easy to remove by vigorous aeration. This can largely be achieved by drawing all brewing water from the mains through a spray device such as a shower head at full pressure. Whatever sprayer is used, it should be well sterilised before taking off brewing water to eliminate the remote risk of problems such as Legionnaire's disease, which can occur in still water. The resultant water is not chlorine free, but low enough in this noxious gas so as not to disturb a fermentation. The water is even good enough for use in malting, which is a process far more sensitive to chlorine than a fermentation.

Simply bubbling air through brewing water overnight using a cheap aquarium pump will have the same effect. Don't forget to leave the lid off and only allow prolonged contact with food grade plastic containers as chlorine could react with phenolic compounds that may be used in some grades of plastics and could produce unpleasant side tastes. But more of that later.

Some homebrewers and wine makers use Camden Tablets, or sodium metabisulphite to remove chlorine. This is total overkill! It certainly works, leaving you with a very dilute solution of sulphuric and hydrochloric acids. At such low concentrations these acids are quite harmless. So where is the objection? Sodium metabisulphite and the like, first produce sulphur dioxide gas that then reacts with the chlorine. Unlike chlorine, sulphur dioxide is extremely soluble in water and consequently quite difficult to remove. So any excess sulphur dioxide not mopped up by the evil chlorine, hangs around to make our water even more unpleasant. Fortunately yeast is fairly unimpressed by sulphur dioxide at low concentrations so again fermentations should not be affected. This is not true when drawing water for malting. Barley, which is our main source of grain for brewing, has to be steeped for seventy-two hours in water before it is allowed to germinate for malting. Never expose malting barley to water containing sulphur dioxide. Chlorine is a harmless friend by comparison!

And let's not get paranoid about mashing with water containing chlorine. Providing we are using the infusion method, the mashing water will be heated to around 75°C (167°F) at which temperature the chlorine is converted into other less powerful oxidants or comes out of solution and is dispersed in your kitchen as the gas. The same is true when sparging, which also uses hot water.

When brewing a beer by the decoction method, it is not advisable to adopt such a cavalier attitude. There may be no doubt that free chlorine gas will wreak havoc with the diastic enzymes at even low temperatures, such as 35°C (95°F), the temperature at which many decoctions start. Provided the chlorine concentration is not too high, one may well not observe any adverse effect but it would be foolish to adopt the "what the eye doesn't see, the heart need not grieve about," mentality. Believe me! We need all the enzyme we can get.

Having said this, I know of one highly reputable brew-pub in Baltimore, whose brewmaster was trained at a leading brewing university at Weihenstephan, who adopts just such a laissez faire stance and argues that a reliable bacteria free brewing water far outweighs any of the problems caused by the presence of chlorine.

Personally I see no harm in giving mash water for a decoction a blast with some fresh air, draw it through a shower head as described above or warm it before mashing.

TCP.

And a final word on this subject. Some brewers are left tearing their hair out because their carefully and lovingly made beers often smell medicinal, of TCP antiseptic one desperate Fred Barnfather of Kent described it.

"What should I do?" he implored me to tell him. "Could it be the yeast that is no good?"

"Stuff and nonsense," I told him with the typical arrogance of a writer on beer who supposed he knew a thing or three about the subject. "You're not letting it lay long enough. It certainly has nothing to do with the yeast."

Well if you are going to be wrong then let's do it comprehensively, is my motto. Fred wrote me again about eighteen months later to tell me he had solved the problem himself. His fermentation butt, purchased from a reputable company, contained some phenolic resin in the plastic. Left overnight with some chlorine containing water, there was an immediate substitution reaction that produced chlorinated phenols, probably some Trichlorophenol (TCP). These sorts of compounds can be detected by taste and smell in a few parts per million and ruined the beer completely. It would of course be quite indefensible of the manufacturers to sell containers for use with food and drink, the plastic of which contained phenol compounds which could leach out. Phenol and many of its derivatives are quite toxic and seriously affect our immune system. Let's hope that such stories are very rare, especially as the blame would be wrongly apportioned. It would be no wonder if home brewing were to get itself a bad name if those in the trade really were guilty of such an oversight. If his supposition is correct, we should all be grateful to Fred for his accurate sense of smell and persistence. This story makes problems such as an excess of insects in one's brewing water seem an irrelevancy! However

Fred may have missed another factor that seems more plausible, for the reputable company that supplied Fred with his container was unable to repeat his experiment, and believe me, they tried! The current thinking on the TCP problem is that it is caused by an unfortunate reaction between yeast and certain hop types. What I can tell you is, that the best dried yeasts and liquid yeast cultures do not produce this problem. Please! Only buy top of the range ingredients.

Water hardness, pH and hops.

Add sodium carbonate to hard spring water to make it suitable to brew with. River, pond, or brook water is best.
(Domestic Brewing. A Handbook for Families. 1843)

Adding sodium carbonate to temporary hard water to soften it certainly works, by precipitating the calcium hydrogen carbonate as calcium carbonate. The trouble is that any excess sodium carbonate will do more harm to the beer and its drinker than the calcium hydrogen carbonate would ever have done. Here we have an example of bad historical practice that we do not want to emulate. The interest here is why so many brewers get quite so excited about their water?

The presence of calcium hydrogen carbonate causes water to have a pH of around 7.5 to 8, and as pale malts have little effect on the pH of a mash, it can be difficult to get the mash pH-value down to the desired 4 to 5 level. Thus, pale beer mashes become less efficient. Furthermore, high levels of carbonate hardness cause certain hop varieties to leave the beer with a very harsh flavour. But believe it, adding sodium carbonate is no solution as in excess it is a laxative and gives water a higher pH-value than it ever had with naturally occurring calcium hydrogen carbonate present.

Treatment.

Traditionally home brewers boil their water to rid it of the carbonate hardness that precipitates out as calcium carbonate (chalk). What a waste of time and money that is? At current electricity and gas prices any sensible house-brewer rejects this idea outright and if your water contains appreciable amounts of magnesium hydrogen carbonate, boiling is not an effective treatment. Adding tiny amounts of sulphuric acid, dropwise is a good remedy as it converts the hydrogen carbonates and carbonates into calcium sulphate, which is generally accepted as an entirely beneficial brewing water salt. This is the favoured method of modern breweries. Furthermore, a slight excess of sulphuric acid moves the pH of the water downwards, which is in the right direction for mashing and fermenting. Where to get a dilute sample of sulphuric acid is another problem. A friendly pharmacist can help. Tell him you want 0.1 molar sulphuric acid with a dropping pipette. He should also be able to tell you how many drips from the pipette make up 1ml of acid. It should be 20. Check this before doing anything rash. A plastic 10ml measuring cylinder costs next to nothing.

Sulphuric acid softening (H_2SO_4).

1g (1000mg) of calcium hydrogen carbonate requires 50ml (100 drops) of acid to remove the carbonate present.

Suppose you have 333mg hydrogen carbonate ions per litre water.

You will need to add 16.5ml or 33 drops of acid per litre of water to remove this amount. Don't forget to prepare at least 5 litres (1½ gallons) of water to mash from.

Before starting you need to know exactly what concentration of hydrogen carbonate ions are present in your tap water and that requires a water analysis sheet from your local water company. In my experience they are always obliging. Look for the columns marked Ca^{2+} and Mg^{2+} and CO_3^{2-} (sometimes expressed as HCO_3^-). These figures show the calcium, magnesium and carbonate ion concentrations, usually as mg/litre, which is the same as parts per million (ppm). Then work on the premise that:

1000mg/litre of carbonate hardness requires 50ml of 0.1 molar sulphuric acid to remove it.

Make sure your water analysis sheet gives the values in mg/l or ppm. These are the most common units but it would be unfortunate if for some odd reason your water company were to use some other variation and you failed to notice this.

Once you have got the hang of using sulphuric acid, you will quickly tire of counting hundreds of drops. Then try asking that friendly pharmacist for some one molar acid. You will only need to add one tenth the amount. Sulphuric acid at these concentrations is not dangerous. Wear eye protection though, wash any skin as soon as you notice a spillage, with soap and lots of water and avoid contact with cotton clothing.

And don't forget to stir the water well during and after adding the acid! pH papers can be useful if you are uncertain about how much acid to add. After small additions (say ten drops) stir the water well and dip in some paper. Read the pH of the water off by comparing the colour of the paper with the colour chart supplied with the papers. Stop as soon as you reach neutral or slightly below. If you over-shoot and add too much acid, then throw that water sample away and start again. We are only talking a few pence here.

If, like me, all this sparring around with acid and pH seems like too much trouble to you, then the only other sensible solution is to brew a beer suitable to your water supply. Here are a few pointers on the vexing question "what beer is suitable?"

Brewing water.

Inspecting the kettle is a good starting point when deciding what your water is like. Even more useful is to take a clean shiny saucepan and boil some tap water in it for 10 minutes. Allow the water to cool and pour some into a glass. Inspect the bottom of the pan by rubbing your finger round it. Is it covered in a powdery white deposit? Is the boiled out water cloudy? A "yes" to either of these questions means you live in an area with a water supply high in carbonate hardness.

Analysis sheets.

If you have a water analysis sheet to hand and you want a general idea of the brewing suitability of your water, then apart from the columns marked Ca^{2+}, Mg^{2+} and CO_3^{2-} which show the calcium, magnesium and carbonate ion concentrations, usually as mg/litre or ppm (parts per million), also study the SO_4^{2-} *(sulphate ion)* and Cl^- *(chloride ion)* concentrations. Compare your results to the table below.

Amount mg/l	Burton	Pilsen	Dortmund	Munich	Hull
Calcium ion Ca^{2+}	294	70	262	75	125
Magnesium ion Mg^{2+}	24	0.72	23	18	5
Hydrogen carbonate ion. (HCO_3^-)	0	27.7	366	310	141
Temporary *(carbonate hardness).*	Nil	low	high	high	medium
Sulphate ion (SO_4^{2-})	801	4.3	240	7.5	40
Chloride ion (Cl^-)	36	5	107	2	37
Action to take	None! Perfect brewing water.	Nearly perfect. Add some calcium sulphate maybe.	Boil or treat with acid.	Boil or treat with acid. Add some sulphate.	Boil or treat with acid.

Gypsum.

The row marked "Action to take," is very tongue in cheek for of course Dortmund and Munich are famous for their beers so why fool around with the water? Far better to brew a Dortmunder or Münchener beer.

Seen from this eminently sensible point of view, one would only ever want to add some calcium sulphate to the Pilsen and Munich waters and this is good news for it is impossible to over-dose water with calcium sulphate (gypsum) as it is barely soluble in water anyway. Burton water is practically saturated.

Most evident in the above information, is that famous brewing towns such as Munich, do not strictly speaking have good brewing water. Nowadays a British brewer would treat Munich water with acid, and before chemistry had revealed the nature of the problem, they used sodium carbonate or boiled the water, assuming they had enough firing material. And before that they didn't know they were getting a poor conversion of starch into sugar and so what the eye didn't see, the heart didn't grieve about. The brewers of towns like Munich haven't had the latitude to use chemistry to sort out their water for nearly the last five hundred years. It was Herzog William IV of Bavaria who in fact passed the very first food quality law in 1516, the so-called Rheinheitsgebot. According to this law, which became generally accepted for the whole of Germany in 1919, German beer may be only made from malt made from barley, hops, yeast and water. They were allowed to boil the water but as already stated, this is time consuming and expensive. To this day they really do have to plough on and brew with unsuitable water. What brewers have long known was that darker beers seemed to do better than pale ones in hard water and so that seemed the obvious solution, and one which I still adhere to today. The fact is that some of the world's finest beers have always been brewed using unsuitable water and despite all the propaganda and hoo haa around brewing water, we can do the same. (The hard water myth is the first of many popularly held beliefs that will bite the dust during ensuing pages.)

Here is a recipe for my house beer, brewed with ground water from the springs of West Hull, being fed by the run-off from the Yorkshire Wolds. As you can see from the data on Hull, we have water with a fairly high mineral content, which is to be expected after it has travelled 20 miles underground from the Wolds to the Holderness Plain. I add crystal malt to the mash because dark malts contain the phosphate ions that tend to pull the pH down and neutralise the effect of the high hydrogen carbonate concentration. It also gives my beers a beautiful red hue that I like so much and which is quite typical of Yorkshire Beers.

Holderness Red Bitter.

Ingredients

Pale malt	*2½ kg (5 lbs).*
Crystal Malt	*½ kg (1 lb).*
Water 5 litres	*(1 gallon) hard untreated Hull domestic.*
Hops	*120g Hallertauer.*

Sugar	*1 kg white granulated.*
Yeast	*1 sachet (7g) Muntons' dried top fermenting.*

Conditions.

1st mash	*Grain stirred into 5 litres of water at 80°C (176°F) to settle out at 75°C (167°F). Held for 1 hour and then allowed to cool to 65°C (149°F) and held 1 hour. Wort run off.*
2nd mash	*Draff stirred with 2 litres (4 pints) water at 90°C (194°F) to settle out at 70°C (158°F). Held ½ hour and run off.*
Sparge	*4½ litres (1 gallon) water at 75°C (167°F). Worts and sparge combined.*
Boiling time	*1 hour. 30g hops added after ½ hour and remainder added after 1 hour. Boiled further 20 minutes. Cooled, diluted to 22 litres (5 gallons) and the working yeast pitched.*
Starting gravity	*1.045*
Storage	*6-8 weeks at 18°C (64°F).*

Enzymes.

The seasoned masher will doubtless be rubbing his eyes at the temperatures employed in these mashes. I have chosen this beer to start with because of its eccentricities and I can't claim that all the beers I brew show such obvious signs of enzymephobia. I do usually give them a fighting chance. But this recipe provides a discussion basis for looking at some more modern-day popular beliefs that have come down to present-day home brewers hewn in metaphoric blocks of stone. I want to subject these common prejudices and practices to a historical analysis. Throughout this book the doubtful reader will be able to find the *raison d'étre* for these seemingly odd brewing parameters. One such prejudice rife in best-selling Homebrew books, is that dark beers benefit from carbonate hardness, and that stouts and brown ales should be the product of hard water areas. The truth is that darker beers are more forgiving of hard water but the best dark beers are also most at home in soft water areas.

Getting down to advanced water chemistry.

Some of us have to consider our water because for one reason or another it is totally unsuitable, but more often than not the real reason is we love messing around and tinkering with ingredients, perhaps in our quest for an authentic beer. The following ideas may help in this quest. To start with though here are a few reminders.

Precipitating calcium carbonate with sulphuric acid, changes the unwanted carbonate to carbon dioxide and water and leaves water richer in calcium sulphate. This latter salt is often deemed beneficial to brewing water. Large plants boil off the carbon dioxide as this gas causes corrosion problems over a period of years but the average house-brewer will not be affected. The main problem is that any excess sulphuric acid that may find its way into the water due to overdosing will severely inhibit enzyme activity. German brewers are forbidden the addition of acids and must draw their sulphates from a biological source such as malt.

PLEASE REMEMBER: Water chemists do not bother to be exact in their terminology. Let's remind ourselves!

Calcium bicarbonate is the old name for calcium hydrogen carbonate. They are one and the same substance. Along with magnesium hydrogen carbonate it gives water its temporary hardness; i.e. hardness that can be removed by boiling. (Magnesium carbonate is actually fairly soluble in water and so although boiling destroys magnesium hydrogen carbonate, it does not remove the carbonate ion, which can be so damaging to brewing some beer types. All other softening procedures mentioned in this chapter do remove magnesium carbonate.)

Names.

When water boils the calcium or magnesium hydrogen carbonate precipitate out as magnesium or calcium carbonate. This is boiler scale and is a great nuisance. Unlike hydrogen carbonates, which only exist in aqueous solution and are therefore invisible to the eye, carbonates can be clearly seen after boiling on the walls of the vessel. Consequently temporary hardness is often casually referred to as "carbonate hardness".

SO! Temporary hardness, bicarbonate hardness, hydrogen carbonate hardness and carbonate hardness do not necessarily mean exactly the same thing but are three names indiscriminately used for the same thing.

Softening with lactic acid.

Lactic acid is a far weaker acid than sulphuric acid and as such will lead the inexperienced into less sin and error when brewing, than sulphuric acid. So brewers who are nervous about dosing sulphuric acid to soften water, should use lactic acid.

Weak acids.

Acids only develop their acidic properties when dissolved in water. Strong acids such as sulphuric acid only have to smell water and they are already up and running, behaving as acids and reducing the pH of the water to around 1. Surprisingly, in the total absence of water, sulphuric acid shows no acidic properties at all but its power to extract water is so strong that only an experienced chemist or laboratory technician should ever use the concentrated acid.

Weak acids such as lactic acid do not fully dissociate and will never achieve a pH of less than 4 or 5. 10ml sulphuric acid in 1 litre of water is totally dissociated into acid whilst the same concentration of lactic acid in water produces only 13% of the acid properties of sulphuric acid. This means that if we use lactic acid to get rid of the carbonate ions in hard water, and we add too much, the excess acid is doing very little harm. It simply dissolves up and then hangs around inertly, taking part in very little. Sometimes a party pooper can be quite useful. In fact the presence of the lactic acid salts is considered to be a useful adjunct when brewing delicately hopped beers and for very pale lager beers it is often added to the copper, rather than pre-treating the water. Because of its harmless nature it is quite safe to add it to the brewing water in small aliquots, stir well and then check the pH of the water with narrow range indicator paper. If you go too far and lower the pH value below 6.5 to 7, simply discard that water and try again.

Lime Treatment.

The most elegant method of treating water is to add lime (calcium hydroxide). Unfortunately it is also the most complex to find your way through without a thorough knowledge of the chemistry of the process so all you brewers who moaned about chemistry at school will now have reason to moan some more. But do pay attention this time round.

Basically the addition of lime precipitates out calcium hydrogen carbonate as calcium carbonate and produces water as the only by-product. The precipitation isn't 100%. About 40 ppm remain in the water but this is only one quarter of what a carbonate containing water would typically hold. Can't be bad? By adding some additional calcium ions in the form of calcium chloride this figure can be nearly halved again. The further addition of potassium hydrogen sulphate reduces the carbonate level even further. But let's not get too carried away! Good Burton brewing water contains in the order of 160 ppm, Dortmund water as much as 270 ppm hydrogen carbonate ions so a figure of 40 ppm with just a little lime looks quite good. Only the water of Pilsen really gets much below this figure. Some Burton water has very little temporary hardness salts, the calcium ion concentration being made up almost entirely of calcium sulphate, which is not considered to be detrimental to brewing.

Adding lime is not such a trial either. Of course it would be foolish not to know approximately how much is needed. 40g of lime will precipitate 100g of calcium carbonate. But a typically hard water will only contain around 300mg/l so we shall only need to stir in 120 mg/l of lime. Assuming we are preparing 30 litres (6 gallons) we would need barely 1g of lime, which is about the tip of a teaspoon full. Too much lime is easily removed. Dissolved carbon dioxide gas readily reacts with the lime and precipitates it as calcium carbonate. If you are worried about having overdosed the liquor, simply leave it to stand for a few hours. Is it still cloudy? If so then the lime is still picking up carbon dioxide, probably from the air. You certainly overdosed in this case. Wait until the liquor is quite clear even if this takes days and then decant the liquor carefully from the precipitate that has settled out. Alternatively discard the water and add less lime.

Take the pH of the water with narrow range pH papers before and after treatment. Calcium hydroxide is such a weak base that there should be no measurable difference in the pH because of a lime treatment. If the pH has risen then you have certainly overdosed so discard that water batch and start again.

The effect of Hard Brewing Water on the Beer.

It is worth considering why we take so much trouble over selecting our water for brewing, or to be more precise, what the effect is of brewing with what we've got rather than trying to mess about and regulate our brewing water. After all, the reality for most of us is that, just like our Baltimore brewer, we take the water from the tap and use it.

Various experiments have been carried out over the years in attempts to quantify the influence of hard water on brewing and nearly all these experiments are beyond the ability of the house-brewer to interpret and certainly beyond the requirements of our craft. One set of historical experiments by E. Moufang (Z. J. Inst. Brew., 1913 19. 242) are appropriate to our requirements. He constructed a variety of brewing waters by adding the correct amounts of salts to distilled water. All values given are in mg/l, which is the same as parts per million (ppm)

Salt/Brewing Town	Munich	Vienna	Pilsen	Dortmund
Calcium sulphate	10	307	282	400
Magnesium sulphate			30	
Calcium chloride				125
Magnesium chloride		24		13
Calcium hydrogen carbonate	307	304		18
Magnesium hydrogen carbonate	106	200	61	
Sodium chloride	5	34	66	61

These waters were used to mash a pale lager malt, first without a protein rest (experiments A) and then repeated with a protein rest (experiments B). There is a staggering difference in the rate of conversion to maltose, the colour of the beer, the amount of extract, the rate of draining of the draff, the acidity and final attenuation.

I quote the most startling of the results below. Lloyd Hind reports that similar results were obtained when the experiments were repeated using a decoction mash and top fermenting yeasts.

	Munich		Vienna		Pilsen		Dortmund	
	A	B	A	B	A	B	A	B
Starch conversion (mins)	75	70	60	60	15	15	10	10
Relative drainage rate	28	40	21	26	08	07	08	08
Wort aroma	v.aromatic		aromatic		neutral		neutral	
Colour	dark brown to red		less red		pale yellow		pale greenish	
% extract	76.5	76.17	7.2	76.6	78.5	77.7	78.3	77.1
Wort and Beer acidity	pH increasing slightly across the table							
Nitrogen	no significant change across the table							
Final attenuation	71	68	71	69	76	74	77	76

You will see from this table that you cannot win. Dortmund water looks to be the best bet but then again the colour and aroma are maybe poor. The starch conversion rates of Munich and Vienna are woefully slow but who cares? We will mash for ninety minutes anyway so we may as well gain from the colour and aroma. The nitrogen and attenuation figures do not alter enough to interest a house-brewer for we are not strictly speaking that interested in a few percent either way. And anyway, a low attenuation gives a high nutrient beer. Alcohol is not everything!!

And here is another thing to ponder. An infusion of malt in distilled water has a pH of between 5.5 to 6 with Ale malts but slightly higher (6 to 6.5) for lager malts. This is very slightly acidic and far more alkaline than optimum diastic activity requires. The figures above indicate that water containing calcium sulphate with a lower (more acid) pH, have faster mashes and that hydrogen carbonate containing waters have slower mashes with their higher, (less acid) pH. The increase in acidity also led to more nitrogen containing material (protein) being present in the wort, although whether the difference is significant may be a matter of opinion. Most important is the fact that carbonates reduce the enzyme activity and therefore are detrimental to the brewing process, no matter what beer we are trying to produce. However, it is arguable that the starch conversion problems that the carbonate containing waters cause are again balanced by the improvement in colour and aroma. I suffer from a fairly high carbonate hardness but find my dark red bitter with a full bouquet highly desirable and as I, like most house-brewers, mash for one to two hours, the slower rate of saccharification doesn't seem to be an issue. Commercial brewers, for whom time is money, will obviously adopt a rational approach to their brewing liquor, and try to tell us that colour is unimportant. This I suspect, explains the marketing drive for light beers.

One can get the best of both worlds by artificially increasing the calcium sulphate content of the water. As indicated, it is impossible to add too much of this salt due to its very low solubility in water. The chemistry of the effect of adding calcium sulphate is very complex but it seems that it converts the naturally occurring alkaline potassium hydrogen sulphate into the naturally occurring acidic variation of this hydrogen sulphate salt. As both these salts are present in malt and one is merely tipping the balance in favour of the acidic version, it seems that adding calcium sulphate to water is an entirely acceptable approach for brewers who wish to increase the rate of enzyme activity. The table also illustrates that apart from the increase in reaction rate there seems to be little else to recommend this procedure of adding calcium sulphate. The slow drainage rates of low carbonate but high sulphate mashes is worth noting, not least of all because drainage can be a painful problem to the inexperienced house-brewer. If hydrogen carbonate ions seem to slow down starch conversion then maybe they are able to speed the breakdown of heavy, sticky nitrogen containing molecules, which may have been otherwise able to block drainage systems. This is pure speculation but certainly more carbonate means more assimilated nitrogen and faster flow rates.

Oddly enough, high carbonate and a protein rest provides the fastest flow rate in Munich water while the presence of calcium sulphate in Vienna water makes the protein rest much of a waste of time as far as drainage in concerned.

We are however now in an area with too many variables and it may be quite erroneous to keep hypothesising. It is difficult to see any other obvious scientific correlation between these two factors though.

Attenuation.

The final attenuation has to be mentioned. We define attenuation as the percentage of sugar converted to alcohol. This value can never be 100% for our only easy way of measuring what percentage has been converted is with a hydrometer. The hydrometer measures the density of the wort and this is affected by all the dissolved material in the wort. Of course not all this material is fermentable and so some will remain dissolved in the wort and unaffected by yeast, so giving a seemingly poor attenuation. Also, when sugar is converted to alcohol, the density drops close to 1.000g/cm^3, which is the density of water. In fact the alcohol formed has a density of less than 1.000g/cm^3 and so makes it appear as if more dissolved material has been fermented than may actually be the case. For that reason we work with the term "apparent attenuation".

This is defined as follows:

$$\text{Apparent attenuation} = \frac{(\text{Original Gravity - Final Gravity})\,100}{\text{Original Gravity - 1.000}}$$

For example, if the Original Gravity (OG) is 1.040 and the Final Gravity (FG) is 1.010 then the apparent attenuation is 75%.

Now the attenuation values from Moufang's paper show that carbonate hardness leads to lower attenuation in brews but richness in sulphate ions seems to counter balance this effect a little. From these figures we cannot be sure why this is. Two possible reasons spring to mind, so we may as well consider them both. The carbonate ions may inhibit the degree of conversion of starch, leaving a greater percentage of large dextrine molecules, which yeast is very slow to work on. This would be in keeping with the very low saccharification figures for Munich and Vienna waters, or the carbonate ions may favour the conversion of large nitrogen containing molecules, (proteins, glutens) and bring more of them into solution. Either way we end up with less alcohol and more non-fermentable material, yielding us a nutrient rich beer; liquid bread as the monks called it when referring to the lent (fast) beers. So let's stop knocking carbonate waters as a matter of principle. We do not have to worry about optimising our starch conversion so we can sit back and enjoy the richer variety of beers that the various waters allow us to brew, at very little effort or expense.

What Water? What Beer? Carbonate Ratio.

Having seen that of the many salts in naturally occurring water, two ions seem to play a major role in a good brewing water, chemists have long sought a method of classifying water by those two ions. One of the most useful for house-brewers is the so called "carbonate ratio". Unfortunately, although water companies will supply you with a water analysis sheet of your water, probably free of charge, not being primarily interested in brewing, they do not calculate the carbonate ratio. Your High School Chemistry will see you through though and you can work it out yourself.

A carbonate ratio of 100:100 is a water containing no sulphate ions so all the dissolved salts come from calcium and magnesium hydrogen carbonate.

A ratio of 100:50 means that there are equal amounts (of moles) of carbonate and sulphate. The actual weight ratio would be 60:96, as the carbonate ion has a molecular mass of 60 and the sulphate 96.

To work out a carbonate ratio one merely turns the masses of each ion into moles by dividing by 60 for carbonate and 96 for sulphate. In the table Burton water has 141 ppm carbonate and 658 ppm sulphate. Dividing 141/60 = 2.35 and 658/96 = 6.85.

If we add these two mole amounts: 2.35 + 6.85 = 9.20.

Now express the carbonate figure (2.35) as a percentage of the total:

$$\frac{2.35}{9.20} \times 100 = 25\%$$

This tells us there is three times as much sulphate present (as magnesium or calcium sulphate) as there is hydrogen carbonate present (as magnesium or calcium hydrogen carbonate).

Put another way, this figure is the molar ratio of $(Ca^{2+}+Mg^{2+}):CO_3^{2-}$.

If the ratio is 100:25 then 25% of the calcium and magnesium salts are present as hydrogen carbonate and 75% present as sulphate.

Now this exercise is only worth doing if you live in a hard water area. We can define hard water as water having total dissolved solids greater than 200 ppm. Your water analysis sheet will have a figure for total dissolved solids on it. (Watch out. Some institutes still use other units such as parts per 100 000). If your total dissolved solids is greater than 200 ppm then it may be worth working out the carbonate ratio. Then you can classify your water into the following types for hard water.

Burton-on-Trent,	Low carbonate ratio.
Dortmund,	Balanced ratio.
Edinburgh,	All purpose.
London,	All purpose.
Dublin and Munich,	Natural dark beer water.
London Deep Well,	Too alkaline for enzyme comfort.

1) Taking Burton as our first example of a hard water brewing liquor, it has a carbonate ratio of 100:25. It is best for brewing pale ales as the calcium and sulphate ions predominate.
2) Dortmund water has a carbonate ratio of 100:60. Here the similarly high sulphate ion concentration is more balanced by hydrogen carbonates. Such water is recommended for medium hopped lagers, which will have a very high apparent attenuation. They will also brew good pale ales but their body will not be so full and sweet as Munich beers. Nor will they have the delicacy of Pilsen beers. Note the high chloride ion concentration, present as sodium chloride. Concentrations much higher than this are to the detriment of the water as far as brewing is concerned although full mild ales can be brewed.
3) The next water classification is the Edinburgh type with a carbonate ratio of 100:70. This is similar to a Dortmund water but with a little more sulphate, not however from calcium or magnesium ions that match the hydrogen carbonate, but from sodium sulphate. Edinburgh is known for pale ales such as India Pale Ale.

4) London water is a typical example of a water drawn from a chalk formation and as such will probably be typical for a great many of us. The carbonate ratio is 100:86 with considerable amounts of sodium and magnesium chlorides and sulphates as well as the predominant hydrogen carbonate ion. This is an all purpose water allowing mild ales and stouts to be made as it comes out the tap, but if boiled and treated with gypsum is good for pale ales. The carbonate ratio of my Hull water comes out as 100:85 with an average chloride ion concentration, almost entirely from sodium chloride. I am very proud of my stout and the pH of the Holderness Red Bitter is helped by the ample amounts of crystal malt that I add (about 17% of the total malt).
5) Dublin and Munich waters are very similar in composition and both cities are famous for their dark beers and stouts. Munich nowadays seems to be the city of pale beers too, but this has more to do with modern marketing and market forces than the suitability of the water and is the best evidence that you can brew the beer you want with the wrong water and still get an excellent beer. The carbonate ratio for Munich water is 100:97 and with a total dissolved solids of around 200-300 ppm, this is considered to be a good balance between magnesium and calcium hydrogen carbonate. Vienna water shows this equivalence too. Furthermore, a boil plus the addition of some gypsum renders the brewer a pale beer water, such as the city is also famous for.
6) London deep well water is extracted by boring through the London clay. The carbonate ratio is 100:124 and warning bells should sound. The hardness cannot come only from magnesium and calcium hydrogen carbonate, but in fact the high sodium ion concentration tells us that far too much sodium carbonate is present. This is a very alkaline salt and although historically it has been used for making sweet stouts it is to be avoided. Fortunately the addition of acids such as sulphuric or lactic will remove the carbonates but will also severely upset the balance of the other salts, leaving the water rich in sodium sulphate.

Caution is also needed when using water analysis sheets, for within a city water may come from a variety of sources. So samples taken from different parts of the Burton area have carbonate ratios ranging from 13 to 39. There can be no doubt that one should specify the street one lives in when requesting a water analysis sheet.

Less satisfactory brewing waters.

If you are unlucky you may find that you live in an area with water that is simply unsuitable for brewing. Certain ions cause pH shifts well up into the alkaline range. Treating the water may be a solution, but I think it is worth purchasing a large water container and importing brewing water from a friend or from work, where they may have a friendlier supply. After all, as we've just noted, you may have to merely draw your water from a different part of town.

The real problem with a hostile supply is that many of the ions cannot be easily removed. There is an ever increasing presence of nitrate ions in our water due to agricultural run-offs getting into ground and river water and only the most sophisticated purpose built ion-exchange resins can remove these. This would be very expensive but be realistic, as unpleasant as nitrate ions from agricultural run off are, nitrate ion concentrations from this source should never become so high that they will affect your brewing liquor.

Nitrates.

Nitrate concentrations as high as 50 ppm are used for brewing pale and mild ales but the carbonate ratio has to be high or else the yeast is adversely affected for with time the nitrate ion is reduced to the more poisonous nitrite ion that forms nitrous acid in aqueous solution. A reasonable level of hydrogen carbonate ions will neutralise the acid. In fact the PCV (prescribed concentration or upper limit) for nitrate ion concentration is 50 ppm and it is very unlikely that a drinking water source will exceed this value. Hull water is getting far too close for comfort to this limit (37 ppm) and is evidence that our water runs off agricultural land.

According to Windisch, nitrate ions have little effect on bottom fermentations until several days have passed, although the yeast may begin to suffer after only sixteen hours with the warmer top fermentations. The upper acceptable limit is considered to be around 50 ppm of nitrate ion although it must be emphasised that many brewers operate successfully at much higher concentrations.

Yeast damage.

The point is to take fresh yeast every two or three brews in order to restrict the damage being done by yeast degeneration. If you are having problems with low attenuation rates then look at the NO_3^- column on the water analysis sheet to see if the nitrate ion may be the culprit. As I nearly exclusively top ferment I never try to propagate a yeast from one brew to the next.

The nitrate ions are usually present as sodium nitrate and as will be seen the sodium ion concentration should be one of our first points of consideration. For example, a high sodium or potassium and a high carbonate ion value but a low calcium and magnesium concentration spells disaster, for if the carbonates are present as the sodium salt, then a very adverse alkaline water will be the result.

Saline water.

Very saline waters with high concentrations of sodium chloride can be used for mild ales and stouts but levels above 400 ppm should be avoided due to the adverse effect on yeast, although there are instances enough of very dark ales being thought to profit by a saline concentration of up to 500 ppm.

Don't despair if you suffer from high nitrate or sodium carbonate levels. Experimentation to find the right balance of dark malts and of hops is a possible course of action that may help. But don't necessarily expect to win prizes with your beers.

Sodium and potassium ions (Na^+ & K^+).

As with all problems caused by an excess of sodium or potassium ions, there is no cheap or easy treatment for saline waters, but they are generally more forgiving for those of us brewing predominantly top fermenting beers. Then the problem may not be acute. 100 ppm of these ions is thought desirable in any top fermenting brewing water and 200-300 ppm is often considered to improve the fullness of the flavour of darker beers. An unpleasant bitterness is associated with this salt when present in well hopped beers. Use of a lower alpha-acid hop is an obvious solution unless you are determined to brew an authentic beer.

Sodium has more to answer for. Although waters rich in sodium sulphate can be used for many beer types, it may influence the flavour of the beer in an unusual way.

Rain water.

Brewers living in a rural area may like to experiment with rain water. This should be very soft, with no dissolved salts and a pH of 7. Industrial areas or homes near to busy roads will suffer from dust and an acidic rain water supply. Such water is not suitable. Assuming clean rain water is available then add salts in small amounts to achieve a good Pilsen water and settle for pale lager beers.

Peaty water.

Many areas of the UK have peaty moorland water and whilst these are usually delightfully soft waters they are sometimes brown from the high levels of organic matter and consequently rather too acid. Probably a cheap active charcoal water filter would help here although the buffering effect of organic acids may make this a waste of time for removing anything but the colour.

Sparge water.

If one is worried about water then of course the most obvious point of correction is the mash water. However, sparge liquor should also receive consideration if you have water with a very high carbonate hardness. The alkaline nature of such water can extract nitrogenous material from the grain, which is detrimental to the wort and as a fifteen minute boil will remove much of the hydrogen carbonate and the water used to sparge is hot anyway, this seems to be a wise precaution. Take care not to sparge with boiling water though, as this can leach all sorts of things from the grain and husk, which wouldn't normally get into the beer.

The actual effect on the flavour of the beer when it is sparged too hot or with alkaline water is probably not the greatest influence on a beer but all sorts of lautering problems may occur and although I'm much more impressed by the flavour of a beer than its clarity, it is nice to drink a sparkling clear beer.

Chapter three.

All about Hops.

Hops and the Water Supply.

And so to hops. Most modern Homebrew literature tells you not to use high hop quantities. My recommended 120g (4 oz) in the Holderness Red Bitter has concentrated some quite hostile criticism my way in the past. Well 120g isn't actually that high and I frequently use up to 150-160g (5 oz) of delicate hops in a hard water brew. The only argument against high hop quantities is that they can cause a very harsh flavour in waters with a high carbonate hardness. All other arguments are pure narrow mindedness. In the 18th century a 22 litre (5 gallon) brew would have attracted 290-350g (10-12 oz) of hops. By the middle of this century these rates had fallen to 70g ($2^1/_2$ oz) for the same amount of beer. Now it is fair to say that tastes have changed, hops are better cultivated and dried now and so contain far greater levels of alpha-acids that produce the essential bitterness in a brew. But even so, the paltry 90g (3 oz) recommended by eminent Homebrew writers (Lines 1974) may sound generous by comparison with commercial breweries but is modest compared with our ancestors. The real explanation is that for many years hops have been an extremely expensive brewing commodity and in the drive to keep costs down, the hop quantities were an obvious target. Now that every small garden owner south of a line from Carlisle to Durham can grow his own hops, there seems to be very little reason not to become more generous again. As for the problem with hard water harshness, this may be another red herring designed to convince us that here and now is the only possible way, and by that justify bad practice. A similar ploy was used in the sixties when some atrocious commercial beers were justified by the breweries by claiming they were only making what the public wanted. The public response was to take up home-brewing in a big way. These then are common marketing ploys that by their very nature all House-Brewers are sworn to combat. So don't be afraid of hops!

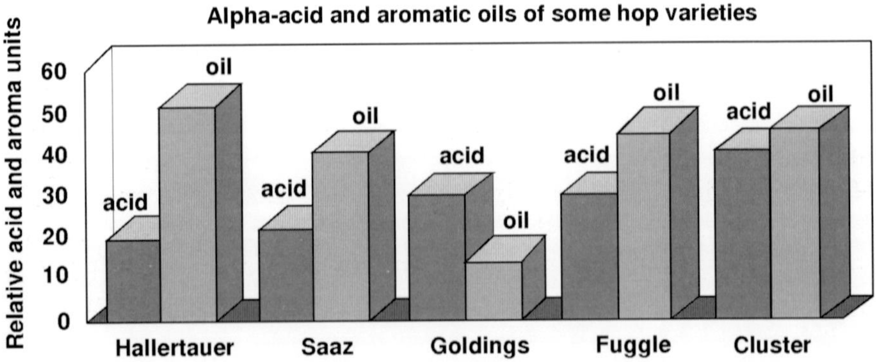
Alpha-acid and aromatic oils of some hop varieties
Relative acid and aroma units
60
50
40
30
20
10
0
acid
oil
Hallertauer
Saaz
Goldings
Fuggle
Cluster

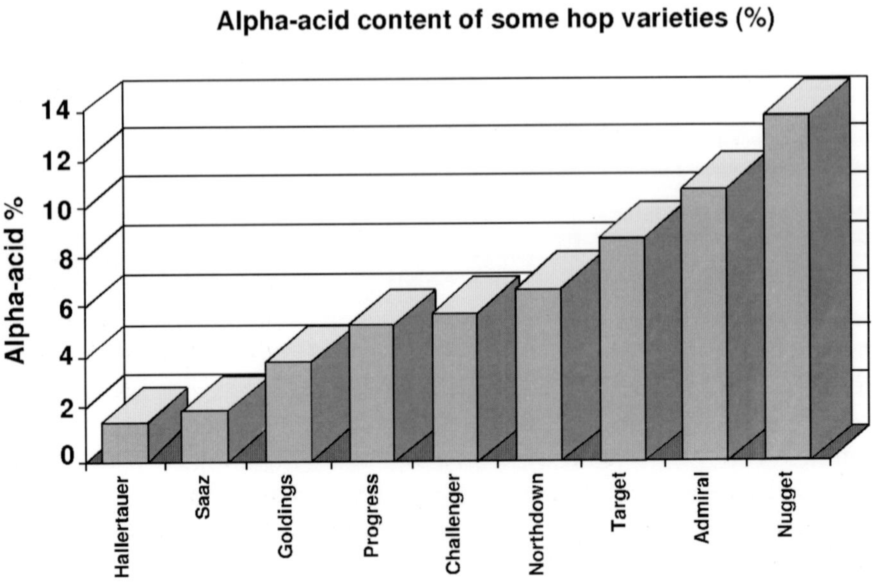
Alpha-acid content of some hop varieties (%)
Alpha-acid %
14
12
10
8
6
4
2
0
Hallertauer
Saaz
Goldings
Progress
Challenger
Northdown
Target
Admiral
Nugget

Of course many strains of hops are quite unsuitable for adding in large quantities because of their very high alpha-acid content but fortunately many hop varieties that are high in alpha-acids and therefore can produce a harsh bitterness, tend to be low in aroma components and vice versa. So if we choose carefully we can use large amounts of a high aroma/low alpha-acid hop, with no danger of excessive harsh bitterness in a high carbonate water. Graphs 1 and 2 illustrate this point and show that the obvious hard water hop is Hallertauer closely followed by Saaz. A full-bodied stout may benefit from a few Fuggles with their more brutal bitterness, if you can get them for they seem ever more rare and lower in alpha-acid. It's all a question of balancing the ingredients to produce what you want.

Boiling.

It goes without saying that high aroma hops do not want to be boiled for the full length of time it takes to reach the hot break, which is usually sixty to ninety minutes. The valuable hop substances are removed from the flower and the alpha-acids begin to be isomerised in appreciable amounts in about 20 minutes and boiling for longer than this merely removes the valuable aroma oils by a process called steam distillation. This is because nearly all organic compounds form constant boiling azeotropic mixtures. As the water boils and forms steam, it carries off the organic oils with it.

Conversion.

Optimum conversion of alpha-acids into the bitter isomerised products occurs between 60 and 90 minutes of boiling time. We see that we have the method at hand to quite exactly control the amount of bittering that the beer receives as well as the amount of aromatic oils left. Addition of a highly bittering hop and boiling for a long time leaves the beer low on the aromatic side. Long boiling of the hops causes high levels of alpha-acid conversion but most of the essential oil is lost through steam distillation.

Variables.

The only way to find out what you like, and what suits your beer and water, is to use trial and error based on the axiom given above. Obviously a note book in which you record every weight, temperature, volume, specific gravity, date, is important. Indeed coughs and sneezes, how well you breakfasted, the air pressure and humidity used to be thought quite essential information. We must not mock. If you are unsure what you are looking for then it can't hurt to record everything, on the off chance you may later need the information. These days we are better informed about what is causing the various things to happen and we can afford to be more casual about note taking. Initially or if you encounter problems achieving your desired beer, do not be afraid to record everything. Just as humid sultry weather can quickly send milk sour so can it upset a fermentation. If your beer is poor or has unpleasant side tastes then a quick scan through the note book may reveal that the air pressure was extraordinarily low, or the humidity high and this can save one the aggravation of looking further for the culprit. The great 19th century chemist Faraday always recorded his mood, his breakfast, even the quality of his bowel movement. Ridiculous? I think not! Brewing, like cooking, can suffer if one is stressed, maybe because someone else wants the kitchen or the floor has just been cleaned and you'll catch hell if you spill some wort, or you are not in the mood or under time pressure. Good brewers are sensitive to that going on around them, but this has its down side. Being sensitive means you'll catch the bad vibes as well as the good ones. - But back to hops!

Bittering.

It is important though not to under-bitter a brew. Taste considerations apart, the alpha-acids present in the raw uncooked hops are not particularly soluble in the wort, do not have the required taste and do not inhibit the growth of the lactobacilli that cause beer spoilage, as effectively as the iso-compounds formed from them during boiling. Therefore it is necessary to boil long enough to form the important iso-compounds and control the amount being produced if you live in a hard water area. This is best done by selecting the right hop variety for your water, rather than trying to get the correct flavour in your beer by controlling the boiling time as the only parameter.

Dry hopping.

Aromatic oils can be added during lagering (storage) if that is thought necessary, by a process called dry hopping as against the more usual copper hopping. Dry hopping is done by a small amount of hops being placed in a sewn cloth bag and suspended in the cold young beer during maturing. There will be no isomerism or extraction of alpha-acids at room or cellar temperature so the bitterness of the beer will remain unaltered, but the delicate aromatic oils find their way into the beer over the course of a few weeks. It is usual to remove the bag after a certain length of time, although there is actually no reason why it should not remain in the beer until the barrel has been drunk. More on dry hopping later.

Rubbing.

The fact that strong late summer wind can cause loss of hop flavouring value by shattering the lupulin glands in a mature cone that is still on the vine, explains the reasoning behind the old practice of rubbing the cones before using them, especially if the cones were being used for dry hopping. It is quite possible that without the heat and swirling action of copper hopping, the flavours will not be fully released during dry hopping. Many old recipes insist that rubbing the cones prior to use was entirely beneficial to the beer no matter how the hops were being added.

Hot break.

In order to achieve the hot break it is common practice to boil the wort as vigorously as possible, which is all very laudable but it does boil off the aromatic oils. Once the hot break has been achieved and the wort has that certain shiny aura to it, turn the heat right down so that the wort simmers, and add another 30g (1 oz) of high aroma hops. Put the lid on and simmer for about 20 minutes, taking care to observe that no appreciable amount of steam escapes the saucepan.

That way the aromatic oils won't be steam distilled off with the steam. Laying a cold wet cloth on the saucepan lid can't hurt the process of reflux. Remember! If no steam escapes then there can be no loss of aromatic oils due to steam distillation. Most brewing advice insists that the more vigorous the boil, the better the hot break and clearer will be the resulting beer. My observation is that the hot break occurs within the usual boiling time of sixty to ninety minutes even if the wort is gently boiled. It must be said time and time again that some historical beers were hardly boiled at all, mainly due to reasons of economy, and the ones that I have recreated have cleared beautifully, had no appreciable bitterness but are so finely aromatic that drinking becomes a whole new experience. And that is what house-brewing is all about.

Hop health.

There is another complication in this gentle balance of objectives! Many of the hops we purchase through retail outlets in the UK have been treated quite rudely by the wholesaler and retailer. Hops deteriorate quickly in warmth and light and loosely packing the flowers in plastic bags is certainly the kiss of death to a good brew. The plastic can form a semi-permeable membrane with a high concentration of volatile oils on the inside and a zero concentration on the outside. This leads to rapid hop deterioration. The alpha-acids also oxidise readily in atmospheric oxygen and both these processes are accelerated by warmth. That is why the traditional method of hop storage is still the best. The flowers were pressed hard into a linen bag, eliminating as much air as possible. If plastic has to be used then tie up the bags and then wrap them tightly in aluminium kitchen foil to prevent osmosis. Then into the freezer with the bags. Do not forget to weigh, label and date the bags. Providing the hops won't be subjected to rough treatment in the freezer, such as a leg of beef falling on them, then the plastic bag is better omitted.

Alpha-acid.

A last word on alpha-acids. As these chemicals provide the bittering in a beer, exact knowledge of the alpha-acid content can take some of the hit and miss out of formulating one's own recipe or trying to recreate someone elses. Some good retailers only deal with vacuum foil packed hops and these will then also have a meaningful analysis of the alpha-acid content. If you are dependent on a retailer then only ever buy such vacuum packed hops. Without knowing the alpha-acid content of hops, all hopping quantities are actually meaningless, which won't stop me from using traditional statements such as "150g Kent hops per 23 litre brew". Of course it won't then be possible for you to re-create that particular beer exactly but I've never found exact copies much fun and they aren't always necessary or desirable.

Foil hops.

Now that we can buy excellent foil packed hops from our Homebrew retailer there is no need to accept those waif-like samples packed in plastic bags, kept at room temperature under bright lights, all of which are deadly to hops. Furthermore, the foil packed hops can be easily transported from all over the world and nearly thirty different varieties are available ranging from super-bittering hops with an alpha-acid content up around 13%, which need to be used with the utmost care if they are not to rip the skin cells from your tongue, right through to the most gentle aroma hops, entirely suitable for use in the hardest of waters or for dry hopping at the end of the boil. The packets tell you clearly what the alpha-acid content is so that you need be in no fear of over or under-dosing.

Formulations and EBU-ing it.

Now that we can know the alpha-acid content of the hops we can get closer to brewing beers like those we cherish most by using the same system of measuring bitterness as the professional brewers do. They use EBU *(European Bittering Units)* and classify beers as follows.

Mild, Brown, Stout, British and Continental Lagers are around 25 EBUs, Pilsners are 28-40 EBUs, Bitter and Pale Ales are 35-50 EBUs and Irish Stouts can be up around 65 EBUs.

There is a simple formula for calculating the amount of hops needed to produce a particular bittering.

$$\text{Weight of hops in grams} = \frac{\text{desired EBU x volume brewed in litres}}{\text{Alpha-acid \% x 2}}$$

Remember! We normally brew 5 gallons, which is 22 litres and 30g is close to 1 oz.

The last red bitter I brewed was hopped with Challenger, a powerful bittering hop with an alpha-acid content of 7%. I wouldn't have dared use this in our hard water without being able to apply the formula. Because hard water can bring out a harsh bitterness I decided to aim at 35 EBUs.

$$\text{Weight of hops in grams} = \frac{\text{35 EBU x 22 litres}}{\text{7\% x 2}} = 55\text{g}$$

Suddenly the hit and miss seems to be disappearing from Homebrew!!

Appendix 1 has some typical alpha-acid percentages for commonly available hops.

Any data on hops will vary from harvest to harvest and will depend on where the hops were grown, so the only reliable figure is the assay printed on the hop bag label. Don't buy hops without a bittering figure if you wish to formulate modern brews. If it isn't important enough for the supplier to find out the bittering figure for you, then that supplier isn't important to you. Hops are very light and mail order is a way round sloppy retailers. There are enough around these days who know their hops. If, like me, you like brewing without exact knowledge of your ingredients, then still insist on the alpha-acid content. That way you know that you are getting hops that have been properly looked after and stored because it is impossible to give an alpha-acid figure for rudely treated hops. Ignoring this figure when brewing is then our personal choice.

Unless you can buy your hops in September (in the UK) from a hop merchant or grower and then immediately wrap them and put them into the freezer, or, you have a retailer who sells vacuum packed hops, you will never have decent hops, unless... unless you grow your own.

Hop growing.

"1 lb of hop dust is equal to 4 lbs hops." (Parkes 1821).

There are many reasons for growing your own hops, price and quality being the two most obvious. It is also great fun and yes, within limits, you can tailor-make your hop to your requirements. This is mainly because ripeness of the flowers and drying temperature also affect the alpha-acid and essential oil composition of the hops. Both of these parameters are under our control.

The disadvantages of growing hops are the space they take up, their hatred of a windy site, their need to grow up to 4 metres, (12 feet) from a predominantly shady nook into sunlight and the fact that they really do not grace a garden once picking in September or early October has taken place. But let us deal with each problem in turn.

The hop has two root systems, one going down deep ($1^{3}/_{4}$ metres or 5 feet) and another set going radially outwards by about the same amount. It sounds like an absolute vandal doesn't it. But it isn't! The roots going down seem to trouble no one and those going outward are only a nuisance because they sprout new hop plants where they are not wanted. These radial roots however do not seem to harm other plants in their immediate vicinity. The tall growing hop will take a lot of light away from the middle of summer onwards so do not plant them close to some other low growing favourite shrub. The hop growth looks quite attractive in summer and forms an effective screen of green, but once this has died back in autumn there is nothing left to recommend this plant. Once you have established a plant it will be there, ever bigger every spring. Don't be afraid to hack it back to the size you want and never allow all the shoots to prosper. If you do, they will take light from each other at the end of the growing season and produce only a few stunted flowers. Five shoots from each plant with no more than two shoots to any climbing path is plenty.

In fact controlling the root systems and shoots seems no worse than brambles or other soft fruits of that type and they do not seem to trouble other flowers or vegetables.

Hop height.

Allowing hops the 4m (12 feet) of vertical height they need is not such a problem as it first seems as they don't actually have to grow vertically and varieties are coming onto the market that manage with around 2½m (8 feet) They will also do very well growing nearly horizontally along wires or through a hedge. I grow mine up an old children's swing and then on into a lilac tree to actually achieve 4m vertically. I don't recommend going for all vertical growth unless you know how you will get the vines back down again in autumn to pick the flowers and unless you live in a wind sheltered area. If you are at all troubled with stiff summer breezes such as are experienced on hillsides or coastal regions, I urge you not try to achieve all vertical height. Even if your garden is fairly sheltered there is no way you can get a frame strong enough to hold the hops and their profuse growth in a stiff August breeze, (especially after rainfall) and have the whole structure look optically pleasing in your garden. We may be talking telegraph poles, which is what a friend of mine in Dublin uses. My garden is not so tolerant and that is why I use the handy lilac tree for the final 2 metres of growth. But even if you think you can secure a frame strong enough, bear in mind that the rough hop leaves will damage each other by abrasion in a strong breeze and the tips of the bine will be prevented from curling around the wire or branch and may be broken off, thus rendering that shoot useless for yield. Wind in August or September is especially damaging to the cones and may result in loss of flavouring. Bruising the cones will cause premature browning to occur. So, as a horizontal solution often offers greater protection from the wind, it may be worth considering even if you have the facility to grow upwards.

The hops will not damage the tree or hedge they grow into and wires angled at a few degrees and ending on a convenient wall or greenhouse, will only need a fraction of the strength of vertical frames. Horizontal bines may have more trouble twining around the wire or string and this increases the labour we need to expend in training the shoots, but this is gentle, uncomplicated work for a summer evening and I never find it a chore. Even vertically growing hops need pointing in the right direction on a regular basis.

Hop Light and Seeds.

Hop plants also like a shady position but want to grow into the light and this is where using trees or hedges or a wall can be handy.

Having chosen a site that will afford shelter from the wind and allow the sort of hop growth that a healthy hop needs, you can start the exciting process of growing your own. Growing from seed is not a preferred option. The seeds from dried hop flowers are unlikely to germinate. This is because most hop dryers in the UK burn sulphur under the drying floors, so that the hops are actually dried in a sulphur dioxide atmosphere. This gives the hops a very even texture and helps prevent mould growing on any unevenly dried flowers, which may retain too much moisture, but it also renders the seeds useless. Continental driers do not use sulphur dioxide in the same widespread manner as English growers, but they do try to eradicate any male plants in order to get seedless female flowers. This is done due to the opinion that seeds only have a negative influence on the beer and as they weigh quite a lot compared with the flower, they are a bit of a waste of time and money. So the only flowers that may contain usable seeds originate in the USA and even here some driers burn sulphur during drying. English growers find that certain hop varieties should contain seeds, i.e. they should have been pollinated and fertilised and to this end they plant male hops at a rate of twenty males to a hectare of females (six to eight per acre). The resulting female flowers are considerably larger and heavier but do not contribute more bittering per flower. In fact the seedless varieties perform better per weight than the flowers containing seeds.

Another problem with growing from seed is that you cannot know what hop type you are growing. The seeds will have the genetic information, and therefore the characteristics of both parent plants. Even if the flower came from a certified Fuggles, but some light puff of air has carried pollen from a distant hop farm or a wild hop growing in a hedgerow, then any hop resulting from this seed will be some unknown mixture of the two. Believe me! Only a very light wind is sufficient to carry the pollen from some hop of doubtful parentage that may be flourishing in a nearby ditch or copse. If fertilised in this way, the resulting seeds will carry the characteristics of both parent plants. As we wouldn't know the nature of both parent plants there would be little point in trying to predict the alpha-acid content and the bittering properties of any hop flowers harvested from such a hop.

Varieties.

By the same argument, it is quite safe to plant different varieties of hop next to each other in your hop garden. The flowers we then harvest will have been built using genetic information from the mother plant alone. Having various varieties of hop next to each other is actually no different from having several varieties of apple tree in the same orchard.

Propagation.

So the only reliable way to start a hop plant is to get hold of some roots. If you live near a hop farm it is very likely they will give you a few shoots during the dormant season in either late autumn or early spring, depending upon when they root divide their own plants. It is worth going into how the roots are divided as it is certain that even small hop garden keepers will eventually want to divide their own stock.

When the plant has finished its growing season, the twines die down to a few inches above the ground. It is this base of the twine that is slightly swollen, which remains alive. This is cut off near the rootstock and used for propagating.

A hop plant always produces more twines than the grower wants. It is therefore common practice to cut the excess ones off, in order to strengthen the plant growth, or to prevent them climbing up the frame and taking light from the preferred shoot. An alternative to cutting them back is to take them and lay them in a shallow trench dug radially out from the root for the purpose. They are covered for the duration of the growing season and then trained up a neighbouring frame when they have reached sufficient length. This method produces a mature, hop producing plant most quickly. Alternatively, this so called "layered bine" can be carefully uncovered in spring and cut carefully at each node, leaving two obvious growing shoots to each piece. These "basal cuttings" should be transferred to the new site and will quickly produce new plants. This root sectioning should be carried out before there is obvious growth. Cuttings can be taken after growth has commenced but the success rate drops off radically and the beginning of May is the last time to consider taking cuttings.

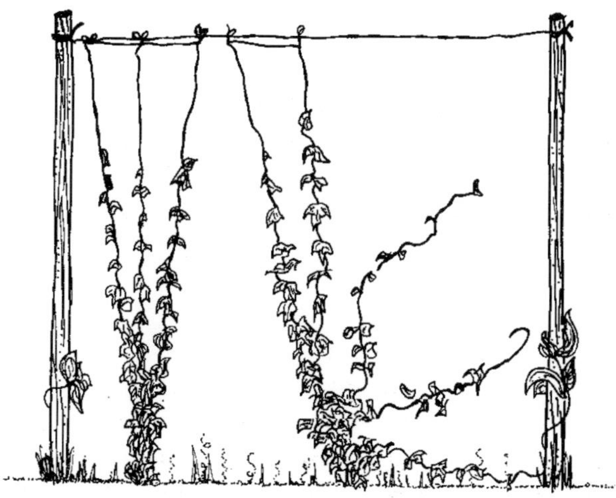

Taking down the Bines: June.

Growth rate.

Where to put the cuttings also has to be mentioned. Hops achieve staggering growth during early summer, managing many centimetres per day.

To achieve this they need plenty of moisture but won't tolerate waterlogged ground.

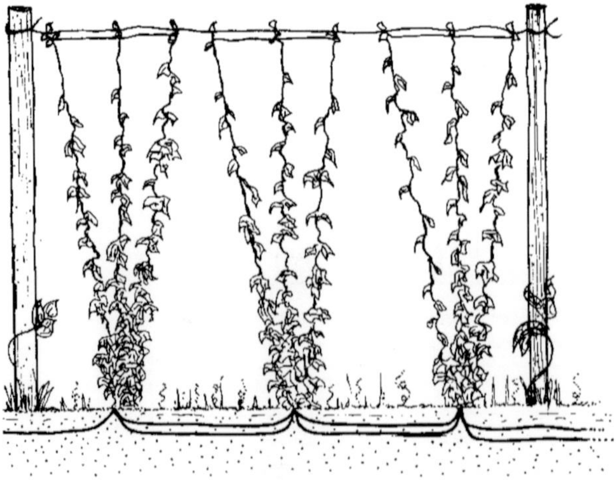

The Bines Layered and Earthed up, July ~ September.

A heavy clay containing loam is best although heavy chunky clay may need a lighter top soil that does drain. Provided the rainfall is adequate they will also prosper in a light sandy soil although a commercial grower would reject this. Most varieties like 50cm (18 inches) of well-drained top dressing. It is ideal if the vertical roots can reach the summer water table but on average a Northern European summer has enough precipitation to make this requirement an optional nicety.

Growers in the US or Australia may have to consider this point though. One of the most endearing features of a hop plant is its indifference to competition from other plants. Some growers encourage grass to grow around the hop plant to improve the structure of the soil. The hop is slowed by competition from cooch or rye but a lawn seed mixture seems ideal, so there is an obvious opportunity for planting hops in or at the edge of a lawn, or in an orchard. The lawn needs mowing with care during the early growing season until the shoots that are to be trained have established themselves.

Disease.

Garden books list plant diseases in a way that often deters a gardener but the manifold diseases that can afflict a hop plant in growth should not cause the ambitious masher turned hop gardener to hesitate. The worst problem that may be encountered is the wind, which, as already mentioned can cause such serious problems that the plant may be weakened and become more susceptible to disease. Do bear in mind

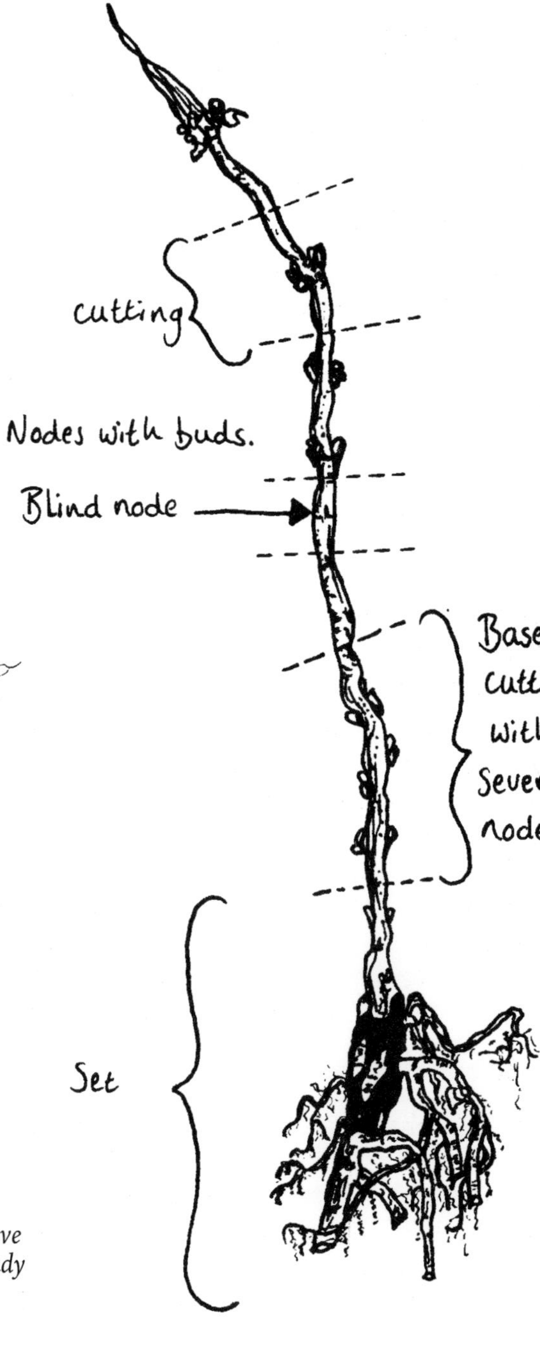

Layered bines can be cut at the blind nodes to leave several shoots on a piece ready for propagation.

that we keepers of a small hop garden will rarely encounter the major problems associated with big commercial mono-cultures.

Picking.

Perhaps the most difficult point in hop production is in the picking and drying, especially as the moment of picking and the drying temperature itself can radically alter the alpha-acid content. This is good news if we fear harshness in our beer from a high alpha-acid crop, for early picking, or drying at a particular temperature, can alter the bittering characteristics. The moment for picking is really a matter of experience, but how we gain that experience without losing years of hop crop during the learning phase is a problem. Here are a few hints.

1) The first sign of the flower is shown by the formation of a brush shaped growth, round and small. In the UK this occurs in the second half of July. They seem to disappear and then reappear with the cone like structure of maturity. The cone develops throughout August and into September. If the brush shaped young flower was pollinated the cones set faster and grow much larger. They are ready for picking earlier. Unpollinated flowers take longer to mature (they wait for pollination) and remain small. Don't discard them as they contain more of the essential oils than a seed containing cone.
2) When ripe, the petals forming the flower are tightly closed making the structure compact.
3) These petals rustle when squeezed and are easily removed from the flower.
4) The petal colour loses its intense green and tends to a yellower hue.
5) The seeds become firm and brittle and have a purple colour, (if pollinated).
6) The hop aroma is strong.

In England this point has usually been reached between 4th and 10th September and waiting longer will only result in loss of valuable hop substance. However you must be guided by the points 1 to 6 for in Yorkshire my hops often need to wait until the first October week

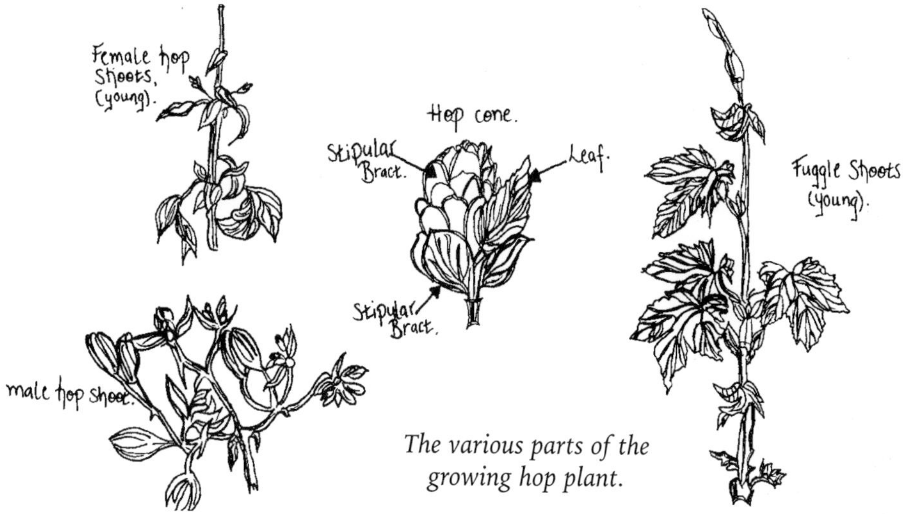

The various parts of the growing hop plant.

to be picked and even in my Mother's Surrey hop garden she waits until around the 20th September before starting to pick. Hop picking should be finished within 10 days of ripening.

Pick the hops by pulling the flowers at a convenient angle away from the stem. This is best done by cutting the plant from its frame, sitting in a sheltered part of the garden and running the stem across one's lap, plucking the flowers with a minimum of force.

A good pair of scissors is invaluable for cutting the chunks of stem into manageable lengths. Do not try to rip the stems apart from each other as this will damage the cones and cause loss of hop dust (lupulin).

In an ideal world we would pick the flowers with the vines still in place and then leave them to die back in winter, returning their strength to the roots. Unfortunately, this is a luxury that vertical growers can't afford. It is far too dangerous.

Air drying.

Drop the flowers immediately into a basket and begin drying them as soon as possible.

If the hops are to be stored for any length of time they must be dried as soon as possible after picking. Many historical recipes demand the use of "fresh hops" and this may account for the huge amounts that used to be used. It is often unclear as to whether they mean fresh undried hops or hops from the current season. This is worth further investigation!

Hops have always been and still are difficult to keep in their prime state and the difference in quality of the beer when it has been brewed with prime hops is unbelievable. We also know that brewers used to use huge hop quantities in their brews. I had always assumed that when a recipe demands "fresh hops," it rightly wanted hops that had not been kept months in warm or light conditions. If we interpret the demand for "fresh hops" as meaning green undried hops, then the large quantities required seem more reasonable for the freshly picked flowers or green hops are 82% water.

It is rare that one can brew with fresh green hops as they deteriorate too quickly if not dried but there seems to be little objection to fresh hopping apart from the danger of wastage due to spoiling. Many herbs, such as woodruff, develop their full flavouring potential during the drying phase, whilst others, such as mint can be used either fresh or dried, although the flavour is fuller when fresh. It has been so long since hops have not been dried as a matter of course that no one seems to know any more to which of these groups the hop belongs. The widely held opinion is that they must be dried before use.

During drying their water content needs to be reduced to 6%. Over or under-drying really won't do. When correctly dried the petals or bracts feel dry and brittle whereas the stalk that joined the cone to the stem, whilst not feeling moist, contains enough water to prevent it snapping through brittleness. One could weigh the moist fresh hops and keep weighing during drying until the moisture content is around 6%, but this is tedious and a large volume of hops cones will need weighing in order to get an accurate measurement from coarse kitchen scales.

Traditionally, the hops were simply laid in a warm dark airy place, such as a loft. In September, a south facing roof of a loft should reach a daytime temperature of around 30°C (86°F) and this, coupled with a light air movement through the loft, may have a thin hop layer dry in about 2 days. This method is entirely satisfactory for modern house-brewers with about 2kg (4 lbs) of wet hops to dry. Larger quantities present other problems but one can leave the cones on the vine until such times as drying capacity becomes available.

There are arguments against air drying at room temperature, which is what I do. The first, and most inexplicable is that room temperature treated hops contain less alpha-acid than hops dried at higher temperatures. I tend to live with this as I'm keen to have a lower alpha-acid content anyway as our water produces sharp resinous characteristics in high alpha hops. This may not be everyone's wish and a temperature of 40°C (104°F) will produce a hop with 50% more alpha-acid. At 100°C (212°F) the alpha-acid content will be 10% lower than at room temperature .

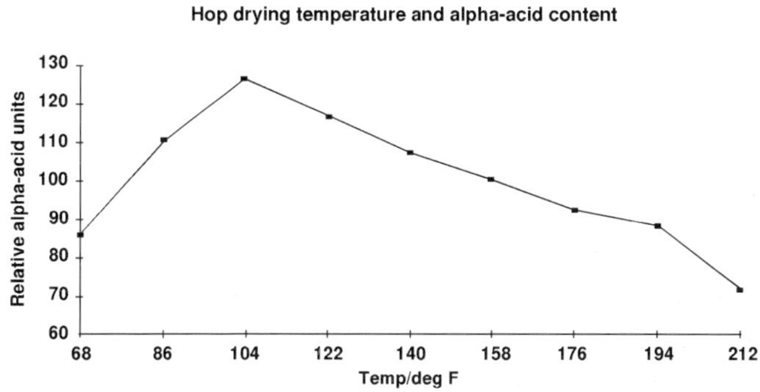

Higher temperatures allow thicker layers to be dried but this also brings with it the need for a fan to move the drying air through the hops, otherwise the hops closest to the heat source or near the surface will over-dry, and those in the body of the pile will not dry at all. An air through-put of around 10 metres/minute (30 feet/minute) is usual.

Although slow and detrimental to appearance, the idea of air drying between 30-40°C (86-104°F) in thin layers seems to offer simplicity and the necessary control over the alpha-acid content that we house-brewers want. Anyone with a south facing roof will achieve these temperatures in late summer in their loft. An air movement of 8 metres/minute, which is a very gentle draught indeed will have a 10cm (2$^{1}/_{2}$ inch) layer dry in 20 hours. Allowing for an inevitable drop in temperature overnight the batch should be finished in 2-3 days. Let the final decision on whether the hops are dry or not be the feel of the stems and petals. The latter should be brittle dry and the former able to still bend without breaking.

Chapter four.

Hop Surrogates

Surrogates.

No discussion on hops would be complete without discussing some hop surrogates and other plants that are used to supplement the hop taste. Since the publication of The Historical Companion, we have had many opportunities to experiment with some of the herbs mentioned in that work.

One of the main opportunities to try out beers of yesteryear is when I'm invited to give a talk to a local wine circle, but three German Clubs and a Christian Fellowship have all requested talks on whacky beers. Such groups are of especial interest to me as many of them are not committed beer drinkers and have tastes that fall outside the run of the mill homebrewer's palate.

Many listeners candidly state they do not like beer. So the challenge is on to see if I can give them something that our forefathers drank regularly and tell them that it is still beer.

My first recommendation is always a Farrenbacher Weißbier, which traditionally only ever had a few ounces of hops in a five-gallon brew. This leaves the way open to beef the taste up with some alternatives. Here are my latest thoughts on brewing this enchanting beer from a recipe at least 500 years old and which tastes like a young white wine and sparkles in the glass like a dry Frankonian. But first a quick word on the meaning of Weißbier. The word Weiß obviously has its origins in the German word for "white".

Over the years this word Weiß has come to be associated with wheat beers, probably because they tend to be very light in colour and nowadays even in Germany a Weißbier is assumed to have been made from wheat malt or a mixture of wheat and barley malts.

The Farrenbacher recipe predates this modern interpretation of Weiß.

Farrenbacher Weißbier

Ingredients.

Very pale malt	*$2^1/_2$ kg (5 lbs).*
Water	*5 litres (1 gallon) soft spring or rain water.*
Hops	*20g Hallertauer.*
Yeast	*1 sachet (7g) Muntons' dried top fermenting.*

Conditions.

1st mash	*Put the crushed malt into a mash bucket with a tap outlet covered by a wire sieve. The mash should be a thin porridge around 35°C (95°F). Run all but the bottom 10cm (3 inches) of this weak wort off through the bottom tap and bring it slowly to the boil. Allow to cool back to 90°C (194°F) and stir it into the main wort. This should now have a temperature around 70°C (158°F). Leave the mash covered and well insulated for around $1^1/_2$ hours.*
Sparge	*9 litres (2 gallons) water at 75°C (167°F). Combine the worts and sparge.*
Boiling time	*8 minutes with all the hops.*
	Cool, dilute to 22 litres (5 gallons) and pitch the working yeast.
Starting gravity	*1040*
Storage	*6-8 weeks at 18°C (64°F) in 1 gallon jars.*

"Experience is your best teacher." (Lord Teynham 1773).

There are several points that can be learnt from brewing a Farrenbacher but it is worth considering why Müller went to the trouble of recording the recipe in the first place. It was in fact in order to be able to point out to his audience how not to brew a beer.

I've streamlined the recipe a little over the years but still produce a near identical product. I now brew it by mashing 2.5 kg (5 lbs) very pale barley malt at around 35°C (95°F) in a mash tun with a lauter bottom for around 1 hour. Sufficient water is needed to make a thin watery mash. One third is then drawn off through the tap beneath the lauter bottom and this liquid is brought to the boil, allowed to cool to 90°C (194°F) and then reunited with the main mash, whose temperature will then rise to around 55°C (131°F). This process is repeated and the temperature of the mash should now reach 75°C (167°F). This is stood $1^1/_2$ hours whereupon the temperature will fall back to around 55°C (131°F).

The beer is sparged as normal but the wort and sparges are boiled together for only eight minutes with 20g (0.6 oz) low alpha-acid hops.

The wort is diluted to a starting gravity of 1.040 and fermented out with a top fermenting ale yeast at around 16°C (61°F). Store the finished beer in a one gallon jar such as winemakers use and cork it well down. It should be ready to drink within a few weeks but will improve with time and may even clear after eight weeks. It tastes best with a sprig of woodruff in spring or as it is in summer.

Everything sounds wrong with this recipe. The low hop quantities and short boil mean that very little alpha-acid bittering is present and so this beer was traditionally difficult to keep. Also, the very short boiling time led me to believe that virtually no coagulation of suspended particles could occur and so I never expected it to clear properly. In fact it doesn't achieve the sparkling clarity that we hope for from our craft made beers but to all intents and purposes, it does clear.

I also serve this beer without any carbonation. It doesn't really taste like a beer anyway and I'm sure that we over carbonate beers these days. I can still remember drinking bitter in a pub in Manaccan in Cornwall that was brewed by a local Helston brewery and delivered in five gallon oak barrels. The old publican would lift his barrels from the cellar and let them settle again behind the bar before tapping and spiling them. The barrel had to be served in an evening for he simply ran the beer out the barrel and allowed air to enter the top. The beer was completely flat but perfectly conditioned, never a hint of sourness and tasted fantastic. He was a true craftsman, very old with a bent back and one of those faces that a lifetime in a beautiful setting, surrounded by beautiful things, had given a unique serenity that quite masked his dependency on tourism for a living. When asked what the weather would be like he always gave the same answer in a firm West Country accent. "My drains b'aint smellin' so I suppose it'll be fine!"

Despite his weather prognosis the deep depressions and rain fronts continued to roll in off the Atlantic but we all stayed on for the beer, his pub being one of the few dry places.

His was certainly not a beer one had to apologise for although it never had that bright shine of a filtered, carbonated beer. Nor for that matter will your Farrenbacher. There is life after gas.

Lautering. (German läutern - to clarify).

My initial feelings were that this beer would never clear due to the very short boiling time that will not coagulate or precipitate out any proteins. It was certainly never clear when I served it to my unsuspecting audiences but I always kept one gallon back to see how it would mature and what its shelf life would be like. Well, it does clear after about three months and it keeps very well indeed, some being six months old when served and still tasting as clean as a whistle.

Woodruff.

How to serve it was another interesting experiment. The beer tasted like a light white wine and had the right colour too. The hop taste could only be perceived by those who knew it was there and so each guest was given a little bunch of woodruff *(asperula odorata)*. The woodruff had been prepared during the last week of April, first week in May, by cutting the low plants just above the ground as their tiny white flowers were about to open. I then tied a few sprigs together, either with elastic bands, green garden wire or wire ties and hung the bunches in an airy room away from direct sunlight until they were dry but not brittle. Some bunches were used immediately by hanging one of them in some light dry white wine poured into a stone jug or pitcher for the purpose. Five minutes or so is usually sufficient to permeate the wine with the exquisite woodruff scent, to make a so called May Punch *(Maibowle)*. Do not throw away the used bunch as it will flavour several litres of wine in one evening, its bouquet improving with use. The same technique is employed with the Farrenbacher Weißbier. I give each guest a small beer glass of the white beer and each table a bunch of woodruff. The woodruff is passed around the table until each glass is flavoured the amount the drinker desires.

The woodruff thus used is supplementing the weak flavour of the hops. Why bother with the hops at all? They do have a disinfecting and conserving effect on the beer and it does have enough flavour to allow it to be served at times of the year when woodruff is not available. Having said that, woodruff does freeze quite successfully by dropping a few dried bunches into a plastic bag and seems to keep well until the end of the summer. By the Christmas of the gathering year its exquisite aroma is still present but the flavour it imparts is no longer good enough to risk in wine or beer.

Lemon Balm.

Another supplement that is a sure-fire success and cannot harm a beer, is lemon balm. This can be added to the beer before drinking, just like the woodruff, or it can be left in the still cooling wort for about thirty minutes, the leaves removed and the beer then fermented and bottled. Here, a word of warning! One is treading unknown territory and it is a shame to risk ruining a beer by spicing it with an unknown herb. Even if we are sure we like the flavour of lemon balm, do ask the question, "do I want five gallons of lemon balm beer?" This is where gallon jars come into their own. Pour the still warm wort into a gallon jar, hang a bundle of the lemon balm in on a piece of string for the required time, then remove it and fit with an airlock for fermentation. This means that five gallons of wort can be treated with several different herbs to give many infusions.

Or perhaps a few gallons should be boiled with hops to yield a safe result. In such instances it is worth using another technique, for herbs such as hops do not have to be boiled with the wort. One needs only boil a flavouring such as hops or tansy with a small amount of water, test the bittering and then add it to the gallon jar. I certainly do this with tansy for although the flavour is good and it bitters the beer nicely, my wife can't stand the smell of it in a beer glass. Another friend can't stop drinking my tansy ale. There is no point in arguing about taste!

Nettle, dandelion and comfrey beer could be your additions to the other gallon jars from a five-gallon mash but again one must use caution. We have essentially lost the art of using herbs and recipe descriptions like "a handful of young nettles" can lead the unsuspecting brewer into all sorts of sin and error. Some recipes recommend dandelion flowers for wine and others the leaves for beer and some do not commit themselves. The flowers can be laid in the warm wort at a rate of one gallon of fresh unpressed flowers to one gallon of beer. Another method is to pour boiling water over the flowers and leave the water standing covered for three days with the flowers in it. This infusion is then strained, simmered again with other spices such as lemon rind and ginger before being added to the wort and fermenting.

The leaves of a plant are more problematic in their use than the flowers. Above all they must be young and fresh. They should be boiled in a little water for around 15 minutes and then strained. Test the infusion by adding a little to a small amount of the sweet wort and tasting it. Do you like it? If so, experiment further with quantities to find out how much of the infusion is really needed in your wort. Three handfuls of fresh dandelion leaves should be enough to spice 1 gallon of wort. Nettles should not be used on their own as their flavour is too harsh unless you can be sure to use only the most young and tender tips. They can be treated in the same way as dandelion. When used without any hops, such herbs or flavours that try to impart a bitter flavour are called hop surrogates.

If all this sounds a bit too esoteric or risky then consider the words of a German beer drinking friend of mine when well down his second pint of tansy Farrenbacher. "Of course German beers are excellent. The trouble is that they are identical in their excellence. This is a genuinely new experience."

Bog Myrtle.

What were beers really like before the introduction of hops in the 15th century? We will never really know as each area had its own special mixtures of herbs that went into various beers in various ways. These mixtures were known as the gruit or more recently named grout. Bog Myrtle or Gale *(Myrica Gale)* is considered by some *(Mathias)* to have been a major constituent, but this bog-land bush has become difficult to find. Grigson believes it was used until quite recently in Yorkshire and the Fens and from descriptions given, it seems to have a narcotic property: "Gave a headiness to beer or ale, fit to make a man quickly drunk" *(Gerard)*. Of course the word beer has many origins; in Old English *(beor)*, Middle Dutch *(ber)*, Old High German *(bior)*, and Old Norse *(bjorr)*. It was the Dutch who introduced the skill of brewing with hops to England so the most likely origin for the name of the hopped drink comes from the Low German word birra, a word reserved by Hythe in 1419 for a drink spiced only with the new-fangled hops. Ale was brewed with herbs other than hops and retained the Latin name for beer *(cervisia)* among intellectuals. Furthermore it was, according to Mathias and Strong a sweet drink, drunk very young and by no means fermented out, and Strong argues that there were instances where no flavouring was used apart from that given by the malts themselves.

In our ignorance of historical reality we imagine that hops ousted the gruits overnight. In fact it took several hundred years before hops achieved the exclusive position we know today. All the while a brewer made a few gallons of beer for himself that would be finished within a few days by virtue of the mediaeval practice of selling the surplus through the parlour window to passers by, there was no real reason to change allegiance from the gruits to hops. As the Middle Ages progressed, more beer was brewed by fewer people and it became necessary to transport the beer, which in turn meant it had to be able to be kept longer. It soon became apparent that hopped beers tolerated weeks in store and a hazardous shaking on a cart far better than the gruit beers. No one seems to have wanted the change on grounds of flavour and most literature up to the 16th century rails against the practice of hopping beer, but the fact that hops produced a more reliable product that didn't go sour so quickly, meant that the economic pressure to change to hopped beers would be irresistible.

Nowadays we need not fear a beer will go off. I've kept unhopped beers over a year in a carefully cleaned gallon jar and as a real ale spiced with gale sounds too good not to try, I've established a wet area in my garden and tracked down a nursery that still supplies bog myrtle. Will it be ready for brewing before this goes into print? Let's hope so.

Spruce beer.

It is also worth asking what the millions of emigrants from Europe used to spice their beers with? Of course many, such as the Pilgrim fathers undertook the hazardous journey only after long and painstaking preparation and they certainly took the most important herbs with them as plants to be propagated in the New World. The majority however had little time to sort their affairs and were fleeing hunger or religious persecution or both. They had only a sack on their backs and had to find new beer spices upon reaching Canada, America or Australia. Some of the more odd solutions to the flavouring problem actually became highly sought after such as spruce beer. This was held in high esteem in this country and the emigrants obviously found a suitable alternative to our native Scotch Pine when they reached Canada or America where spruce beer was soon to enjoy an enviable reputation.

When Scotch Pine was used the fir tops and rinds of a tree similar to the common Scotch Fir *Pinus sylvesteris* were said to be infused. The Canadian or American beer was made using *Pinus Nigere* or Black Spruce. This is a native of US and probably used long after the first Spruce Beer had been made by the Germans, who are reputed to have been the originators of this drink. All species of fir have more or less the same resinous principle that preserved the beer from that ever present hazard of acidity. *Vina Bicata* was a wine spiced with fir, made by the Romans and which was held in high esteem for this reason. Its antacid properties were still taken advantage of by the brewers of Augsburg in the middle of the nineteenth century. Here is an eighteenth century version of Spruce Beer.

Brunswick Spruce Beer.

The *Encyclopaedia Methodique* states:

"The French residents of Canada make their spruce beer by first boiling the small shoots, chips, leaves and cones in water, then adding to the liquid the roasted meal of either rye or barley. When a beer better than ordinary is required they use maize, which is preferred to any other meal.

When this decoction is cool it is fermented with yeast. An addition of sugar syrup is made to cover the resinous taste, (presumably added just before drinking or else it would ferment out). The beer is reputed to be fit to drink in 24 hours after fermenting, (so it wouldn't have had much chance to go sour).

Roasted grain gives the beer a beautiful colour and by adding body, rendered it more agreeable and nourishing. It soon becomes clear and when poured, froths like any other beer. The beer is diuretic and keeps a long time, without becoming acid in warm weather."

Common Spruce beer.

Common Spruce Beer of this country is, according to the anonymous author of *The Art and Mystery of Brewing,* made with the essence of spruce fluid extract, which could be procured in large oil shops or in chemists in small stone bottles during the nineteenth century.

"It is prepared by boiling the twigs sawn off a Scotch Fir.

To make the beer, procure the essence of Spruce.

4 gallons of boiling water are poured into a cask with 4 gallons of cold water.

This gives proper heat to the whole. (A temperature of 30°C (86°F) would seem about right so their cold water may have been barely above freezing).

Then add 8 lbs treacle and 2-3 tablespoons of the essence.

Stir and add ° pint good yeast.

Keep temperate until fermentation lets up (48 hours) and then bottle. It is fit for use in 2-3 days."

This beer is also of interest as it requires no malt at all and uses that most berated additive to beer, sugar. More on sugar beers later.

Chapter five.

All about Malt.

Altering malts and nitrogen content.

Another genuinely new flavour experience can be found by malting different grains. But it is not only the variety of beers that become available by malting at home that make it important for us to add malting to our house-brewing chores. By buying from our local Homebrew retailer we have no control over the type and quality of barley that is actually used to make our malt. I've long suspected that the Homebrew trade gets the hops and barley that are considered too substandard for the professional brewer to entertain.

Homebrew malt is certainly ground too fine and too long in advance of us brewing. Good brewer's barley for instance should not have a dry nitrogen content of higher than 1.2 to 1.4% for an all grain beer. If sugar or some other grits are to be also fermented, which contain no nitrogen themselves, then it is permissible to use a higher nitrogen content barley, in the range 1.5 to 1.7% dry weight. Dry weight nitrogen values above this range do not malt well and below 1.2% may not provide enough nutrient for the yeast to successfully work. Do you know your barley nitrogen content? Of course not! Some wort concentrates supplied in cans are reluctant to ferment out and retain an undesired sweetness. Perhaps there is too much sugar present, which lowers the percentage nitrogen below the acceptable minimum, or too much nitrogenous material has been deliberately precipitated out by the manufacturer so that the beer will clear quickly.

The actual nitrogen content of the grain depends to a large extent on factors over which the farmer doesn't have a great deal of control. Of course he plants seeds of a variety reckoned to give him the best required nitrogen content, but barley grown on sandy soil or fen-lands may well produce high nitrogen as will a poor tilth and late sowing. The latter two factors often depend on the weather. Before the farmer can sell his crop he has to pay for an analysis that will probably tell him the protein content of his crop expressed as a percentage of the total weight. On average protein molecules are about 16% nitrogen. So the minimum protein percentage should be 7.5% and the maximum for an all grain brew about 8.75%. As much as 10.6% nitrogen is allowable for beers that will contain fermented sugar or other low nitrogen grits.

Farmers who end with a protein percentage of 12 or 13% will get very little for their crop. Maltsters will still buy it, malt it and sell it to the Homebrew trade, as we are the only brewers who do not demand a nitrogen or protein content assay.

Professional craft-brewers don't get it all their own way either, and are often as dissatisfied with the malt they are sold as the house-brewer should be. The famous Swiss scientist and brewer Fritz Schoellhorn insisted on malting barley on the premises for the premium Haldengut Pilsner.

He invested huge sums in his own malting and only stopped malting when the beer market collapsed with the advent of the 1914-18 war. Just prior to that the Haldengut Brauerei was brewing over 100 000 hectolitres per year and their malting could cope with six metric tons of barley per malting. But whereas they could demand a chemical assay, or carry one out themselves, we are left in the dark.

Barley.

"Wheat requires longer malting, oats shorter. Peas, beans and maize according to fancy." (Levesque. 1836).

Barley has the foremost position as a malting grain and will probably always retain it. Wheat is more difficult to malt because it doesn't have the protective husk, which keeps the acrospire safe and well. Thus the act of turning the malt on the floor as it is germinating, tends to ruin the wheat.

There is no alternative to turning on the floor because it is the only way to prevent the roots of the growing grain from becoming an impenetrable mass of intertwined material. Once this happens it is almost impossible to break apart again but if left in that state, will produce very unevenly grown malt, much of which may be actually ruined through being exposed to localised hot-spots.

Oats.

Beers made from oats are always highly praised, but despite claims by some writers that oats can be malted in the same way as barley, it took me several attempts before I succeeded. This is probably because I've yet to understand what these 18th and 19th century writers are really trying to tell their reader. This is just one of the joys of historical research when words and ideas have changed their meaning over the years. The unknown author of *The Art and Mystery of making British Wines* also *The Whole Art of Brewing (1865)* uses expressions such as "take malt of the right description," for a Yorkshire oat ale, so as late as the middle of the last century oat malt could be purchased from the grocer's shop.

Steeping.

My initial oat malting difficulties were caused by the statements in the literature such as "malt oats as you would barley." Now the first step in malting barley is to steep it in water at 8°C (46°F) for 72 hours by which time its water content will have increased from 8% to 40%. Barley is totally reliable and indeed always takes 72 hours at 8°C to achieve this remarkable feat. The oat grain is however much smaller and made up of much less corn substance so the key here is to go for the right weight increase, not be looking for a 3-day steep. In fact oats have the correct water content after 12-18 hours at 8°C (46°F), which makes them an obvious choice if time is limited.

There is no measurable water uptake after this period whereupon the grain is approximately 33% water. The water must be aerated with a small aquarium pump and changed twice a day to prevent the grain suffocating on its own carbon dioxide *(Historical Companion, pages 86-88)*. When the correct water content has been reached, the wet grain is dried of its surface water by hanging in a sieve or bucket with its base perforated with 3mm ($^1/_8$ inch) holes. A stream of damp air should flow up through the grain until the first roots appear.

Germinating.

A germinator made from two buckets is indispensable at this point. The top bucket with the perforated base fits tightly inside the lower bucket, which contains a few inches of water. Air is pumped down through the grain using a piece of plastic aquarium tubing. The end of the tubing passes through one of the perforation holes enlarged for the purpose and goes on into the water. Weight the end with a piece of lead to keep it under the water. The air now saturates itself with water and then passes back up through the grain, and so prevents drying out. Our grain still needs turning at least twice daily and should be kept around 12°C (54°F). The internal temperature may not exceed 16°C (61°F). If this looks likely to occur, then turn the grain more frequently to allow the heat to escape.

When the first roots appear as tiny white eyes in the base of the grain, it is time to restrict the amount of air getting to the corn. This way one prohibits the growth enzymes that are responsible for turning the corn starch into energy giving sugar from wasting too much starch. The corn though, is encouraged to continue to produce enzymes, which is what the brewer wants. So now is the time to suspend the sieve or bucket from a nail or a purpose built wooden frame and so allow some of the heavier carbon dioxide gas to escape, at the same time drawing fresh air in through the top. The amount that actually escapes is regulated by covering the sieve bucket with a lid and so allowing only a restricted movement of carbon dioxide gas downwards through the holes.

Turning.

Still turn the grain twice daily to prevent heat buildup and root matting. 12-16°C (54-61°F) is the correct temperature within the body of the green malt. 20°C (68°F) should never be exceeded.

Regularly take a few grains and gently peel back the husk on the swollen growing corn. With care and a magnifying glass if one's eyesight is beginning to fail, one can find the acrospire or green shoot. This should not be allowed to exceed two thirds the total length of the grain. When it has reached this critical length, the grain is ready to be dried. It is the removal of the water that causes the enzymes to again become dormant but unlike the winter sleep of dry cold grain, from which we can wake the seed with warmth and moisture, we actually kill the germinating plant, leaving only the enzymes intact, ready for use by the brewer to convert the remaining corn starch into maltose, ready for fermenting.

Drying.

Oat malts were only ever dried to yield a very pale malt and to this purpose the so-called green malt is laid out thinly in a warm dark airy place at about 30°C (86 °F) and left until its water content is down to around 2%. Bag it up in plastic and store until required.

Even if dark malts are required the malt has to be dried before roasting. Any heat above 45°C (113°F) will destroy the enzymes in damp malt. Once dried to about 8% the enzymes will remain intact up to temperatures of around 75°C (167°F). Above 90°C (194°F) the enzymes will suffer and the starch will begin to show signs of browning. Once the starch becomes brown it loses its typical polysaccharide structure (lots of glucose units linked in a chain) and can no longer be broken up as well by the enzymes. Enzymes are like keys. Damage the lock and the key won't work. This means that damaged starch molecules will not become fermentable maltose (a disaccharide). Such brown starch will give the beer colour, flavour and a different body but little alcohol.

A complete set of drying and roasting charts for a variety of malts is to be found in *The Historical Companion to House-Brewing pages 90-92*.

If you can't get some fat unrolled oats then skip the next recipe, and try my oat ale using rolled jumbo oats from the health food shop with a little malt for enzyme supply.

Yorkshire Oat Ale (1865).

This beer was originally reputed not to keep in summertime but modern sterilising solutions seem to have cured that unfortunate ill. The malt should be crushed, not ground. And the taste? Rather like cider but I mean proper cider with a suspicion of hops.

Ingredients.

Pale oat malt	*2½ kg (5 lbs).*
Water	*5 litres (1 gallon) cold soft water.*
Hops	*100g Goldings.*
Yeast	*1 sachet (7g) Muntons' dried top fermenting.*

Conditions.

1st mash	*The grain is stirred into 5 litres cold soft water.*
Sparge	*Run the water off in a small stream and infuse with the well-rubbed hops for 3 hours. Strain off the hops.*
Fermentation	*Run the wort into the fermentation vat and ferment out in around 3 days. Stopper loosely and keep 10-12 days and then bottle the ale.*

Under these circumstances the enzymes are activated as the grain takes up water again and then starch conversion to sugar can commence.

Most modern brewers would doubt the sense of mashing the malt in cold water for long periods but the oat malt has sufficient enzyme content to do the works at low temperatures. The above recipe is also interesting as it relies entirely on dry hopping for its flavour.

Dry hopping used to be widely practised in the UK and still has many friends in the United States, where some of their most cherished crafted beers are so strongly dry hopped that the taste of the beer is quite astringent. Unlike the oat ale recipe that I have given here, the American method consists of boiling the wort with a high alpha-acid hop for 60 to 90 minutes with the addition of an aromatic hop towards the end of the boil. Then, during the lagering of the beer, the so called dry hopping takes place by adding some highly aromatic hops to the young beer. These are left in the young beer for around two weeks and if a muslin bag is used to hold them, they may be easily removed before the keg is brought on line. Dry hopping in this way provides no additional bittering to the beer but gives it a highly aromatic flavour that the so called "Hop Heads" of the East Coast cherish. The same effect can be achieved more conveniently by dry hopping during fermentation and removing the hops before kegging. Traditionally, dry hopping included a barrel roll to prevent a concentration build up near the hops, hindering the diffusion of the aromatic oils into the beer. The barrel was simply turned on its side and rolled back and forth a few times.

Everyone wants a good rolling boil in order to achieve the hot break as effectively as possible by causing the suspended solids to collide with each other most vigorously and thereby coagulate, but it is this hard boil which produces so much steam and causes the aromatic hop oils to steam distil from the wort in a matter of minutes. One could condense the steam before it leaves the boiling copper and thus reflux the water and hop oils back into the copper but this is not an option. Some of the hop compounds have to be removed from the beer by steam distillation. Careful regulation of the heat input to your copper however, is most important for it is possible to achieve a vigorous boil and limit the amount of steam leaving the copper but still remove some of the unwanted oils.

When the boil is finished and the heat turned off is a good time to add the aromatic hops. There is hardly any steam escaping but the wort is still hot enough to effectively leach out the aromatic oils. This method of "cold hopping" seems to reduce the astringent taste that characterises so many American beers, should it not be to our taste. One does indeed grow to love that very taste, so for those of us who want to try it out here is a typical American dry hopped beer.

Hop Head Ale.

Ingredients.

Lager malt	2½ *kg* (5 lbs).
Pale malt	*1 kg* (2 lbs).
Crystal Malt	½ *kg* (1 lb).
Cascade hops (5.4% alpha-acid)	*8g* (¼ oz) *60 minute boil.*
Crystal hops (3.5% alpha-acid)	*60g* (2 oz) *60 minute boil.*
	15g (½ oz) *30 minute boil.*
	8g (¼ oz) *10 minute boil.*
	8g (¼ oz) *dry hops.*

Special London Ale yeast from Wyeast was used.

Data.

Original specific gravity	*1.055.*
Final specific gravity	*1.014.*
Total boiling time	*60 minutes.*
Primary fermentation	*14 days at 20°C* (68°F).
Secondary fermentation	*14 days at 18°C* (64°F).

This recipe won a prize at the 1994 American Homebrewer's Association national competition under a different name. I've had to alter it slightly to include more easily available ingredients, but you'll quickly observe that the emphasis is quite different to UK recipes. No mash times or temperatures are given. No volumes of mash and sparge water appear. The entire emphasis for flavour is on the hop types, boiling times and the fermentation. There is obviously a whole new world of brewing out there, which us Europeans have never considered and have yet to discover. No value judgements please!

Compare the hopping procedures of this Hop Head Ale with our very traditional oat ale. Our oat ale relies on no more than the wort being run through and over some dried hop cones. Again these have to be of an aromatic variety, (Saaz or Hallertauer) and even then only a suspicion of flavour will show through, which makes them an ideal vehicle for light summery herb beers dry spiced with woodruff or lemon balm. The hops used for such a brew were not discarded but used for copper hopping the next brew. I suspect that in our nowadays times of plenty, such parsimony would find few friends. Shame!

But a major problem with such beers in which the cold wort is run over a few dried hops is that they will not keep as well as we nowadays expect a beer to. The 19th century writers advise consumption within two weeks and this has two reasons. First, this recipe omits the boiling of the wort and so no final sterilisation process is included before fermentation, and secondly the absence of alpha-acids in the wort shortens the shelf life of any beer. It was, after all, the realisation that hops increased the keeping qualities of a beer that ultimately secured them as the beer flavouring of the last 400 years.

Here is my more modern version of an oat ale that will keep several months and doesn't require the oats to be malted first. There is historical evidence that such unmalted oat beers were also brewed.

Clive's Quick and Sticky Oat Ale.

Ingredients.

Pale malt	*½kg (1 lb).*
Crushed Jumbo Oats	*1½ kg (3 lbs).*
Water	*5 litres (1 gallon) soft or rainwater.*
Hops	*30g (1oz) Goldings.*
OR	
Tansy	*1 cup of young leaves.*
Sugar	*1 kg (2 lbs) white granulated.*
Yeast	*1 sachet (7g) Muntons' dried top fermenting.*

Conditions.

1st mash — *Mix the oat flakes and malt to a thick porridge around 35°C (95°F) and stand for 2 hours to allow some protein to be broken down.*

Slowly add boiling water with vigorous stirring to bring the temperature up to around 55°C (131°F). Stand for 1 hour.

Ladle about one third of the content of your mash bucket into a saucepan and bring it carefully to the boil making sure it doesn't burn. Return the hot saucepan mash to the main mash and the temperature should get up to around 70°C (158°F)

Sparging — *Sparging oat ales is not a task to be lightly undertaken. Unless the weather is particularly inclement I advise you to retire to the yard, or else stand all your sparging equipment in the bathtub. If you feel the kitchen is the only place then prepare your spouse for house-brewer's syndrome: that aggravating complaint where your shoes become reluctant to follow your feet. Sparging oat ales is indeed a very sticky business. Here we go!*

Ladle off as much liquid as possible back into the saucepan. Mix more boiling water into the draff to give a thin consistency, stir gently for 15 minutes and then ladle off the water or strain through a colander or loosely woven

	cloth. Oats are rich in thick sticky glutens and they seem to run out the draff for as long as you are prepared to sparge. When your total mash and sparge volume is around 15 litres (3¼ gallons), stop sparging. Don't worry about a few grains ending in the wort.
Finishing off	*Add any sugar intended, and boil the hops and/or tansy for around 15 minutes.*
	Ferment right out with a top fermenting yeast at around 18°C (64°F). Rack into bottles or gallon jars.
	If tansy has been omitted (it is definitely an acquired taste) and it is the right time of year, this beer is another perfect vehicle for serving woodruff or lemon balm.

Rolled oats.

I'm sure that some purists may be disappointed by a book on historical beers advocating the use of rolled oats, (which wouldn't germinate anyway), being mixed with a bit of malt to provide the enzymes and then being mashed to make a false oat ale. Let me justify the second ale by telling a little story, which may or may not have happened. I'll let you decide that.

When I started researching the history of brewing, especially trying to recreate beers that had not been brewed in hundreds of years, I assumed with the folly and arrogance of youthful ignorance that times past were the ages of good pure wholesome unadulterated beverages. Like Hell it was! An equally apt title to this book would have been to steal the words of the song, "Anything Goes". Homebrewers one hundred years ago had to be far more resourceful than we are today. There was no homebrew retailer in the high street with a complete and seemingly never ending supply of ingredients. And five hundred years ago there was no guarantee of anything in the brew shed. There were no holy cows in the world of historical brewing when the chips were down.

A brewer's parable (1645).

If the barley harvest failed then that was the end of the story. No beer!!! Unless... Unless you were prepared to use whatever was at hand. If the barley harvest failed but the oats were good, then you looked your horse square in the eye and told him whose needs were the greater. If the hops had an irreversible blight then how about seeing what else in the field was bitter and aromatic. And then twenty years later when reminiscing about the "good" old days someone would mention in a haze of nostalgia how grand that ale had been back in forty-five when the barley failed; and how we'd all pulled together and made the most fantastic oat ale ever, spiced with bog myrtle, and how no one had been able to sleep nights for the rumbling in the horse's belly and wouldn't it be grand if we could have a beer like that again?

Of course the true answer would have been "NO". Forty-five had been a terrible year of war and pestilence and the less said about it the better but in 1695, just like now, one only really remembered the good times. The bad bits fade into a distant mist and some fool says, "Let's brew another oat ale."

Everyone is enthusiastic. The oat harvest that year had never been better and there was plenty of bog myrtle again in the long swamp.

And then comes the sad realisation that the old mash tun and pump have been thrown away so it can never be exactly as it was in forty-five and worse still is that in the intervening years it has become custom and practice for the groom to bruise all the oats for the winter so they won't germinate anymore and no one can steal them to make beer. One can't really blame the groom. After all, his father it had been who had got it in the neck in forty-five when the horses were all bad tempered and too weak to do any work.

The old squire by now is in a foul temper and shouts at his wife. He'd always said they should keep the old mash tun. So what if it had leaked in fourteen different places. How much he had looked forward to recreating the days of his youth and how bitterly disappointed was he when he realised that his wife has ruined it all by chopping up the mash tun for firewood. He storms out, slams the door, breaking two hinges, and goes off to find the groom to give him a good beating. His wife is unmoved. As she remembers the story of forty-five, he had moped and moaned all autumn about the barley harvest, and she had done all the work and made enough ale from oats to get them through the winter and what a sticky sordid mess that had been. They had been forced to hire extra labour just to pump water to try and keep the flags free of that awful sticky gluten that the oats seem never to stop oozing.

But her daughter is more conciliatory. She may have no memories of the oat ale, but knows by heart all the stories she has heard around the hearth about the oat ale back in forty-five and wants finally to try and recreate it. It seems to her that her whole childhood was dominated by stories of that damned oat ale. Finally she wants to try one. And it is only natural to her that it should be the women folk who think of a way of making a new oat ale with bruised oats that will taste like *(or better than)* the forty-fiver, so that harmony can finally be restored to the household. Of course the women can manage such a task because they are keen observers and have a natural feeling for their ingredients and process. This had to be so if they were not to starve in times of dearth when every goose quill, every acorn had to be harvested and preserved for some purpose.

Fortunately for us, one granddaughter could read and write and because she wasn't allowed to help because she wasn't there in forty-five, nor was she round the hearth in the ensuing years when the yarns about that great year of adversity were spun; she sits and watches and records both recipes, the original and the recreated ale, just for fun and to try to be part of everything. And how eternally grateful we should be to her, except we no longer know which recipe we should consider to be authentic.

Chapter six.

Brewing Techniques.

Shock cool.

When I first started making oat ales, which were dry hopped with no boiling time, I assumed they would never clear properly. As I said, they were recommended to be drunk within a few weeks of brewing so under those circumstances they certainly didn't clear. It is the boiling of the wort that swirls around the suspended particles causing them to collide and hopefully stick together. As their particle size increases under this treatment so does the chance that they will settle out of the wort as it cools. Rapid cooling of the wort after boiling further encourages even the smallest suspended particle, as well as much dissolved material, to precipitate out in the so-called cold break. Some European and American brewers shock cool the beer during secondary fermentation as low as 2°C (36°F) to maximise this precipitation, and so to ensure they get a really clear beer.

Hot break.

Obviously if we don't boil the wort then we cannot expect this important coagulation to take place. Nor can we expect the alpha-acids to isomerise and bitter the beer.

Now many historical writers maintain that every beer clears eventually and this has certainly been my experience. Even the stickiest oat ale has cleared after eight weeks in store, and now that we have sterilising solution readily to hand we can risk keeping an unboiled beer that long. Personally I would always bring it to the boil for just a few minutes though to sterilise it. Yes! This will alter its nature slightly, but I find it quite soul destroying to have to dump a beer down the drain because of some wild fermentation. Worse still is the fact that once you have allowed a beer to become sour, you have also allowed the bacteria, which caused this sourness to establish themselves in your brewhouse. Even with modern sterilising solutions, this is a dangerous path to tread. In my quest for some oddball beers I came across the following recommendation by that much maligned nineteenth century brewer Mr. Richardson. Perhaps his critics were right!

Hard ale.

"To make recently brewed ale stale, or become hard, add to a barrel of new ale, 1-2 gallons common vinegar or ale, which has become naturally hard with age. The Ale to be changed must have discharged the greater part of the yeast, and so after cleansing, fill the cask to full, stop down close that a violent internal vinous fermentation may ensue, otherwise the effect may not be perfect. Let this continue 3-4 weeks with no other vent than the stopper, which may be thrown out (by the vinous fermentation). After this time finings are added and the ale is then fit for use. Sometimes hops are used, sometimes not."

Old Ale and Sour beer.

Easterly winds are bad for brewing and worts exposed to them rarely escape injury. The sweet wort will often contract and acidity not to be eradicated. (18th century brewer's aphorism).

Our sour beer description gives a new meaning to recipes for Old Ale. Were these very popular and sought after beers actually allowed to turn "foxy" because that was how a certain type of drinker wanted them?

Not wishing to leave any stone unturned and because I'm sure the ancient Egyptians drank their beer sour more often than not, I allowed the end of a barrel of a beer to "naturally harden". I then brewed another ale to add this hard remainder to. I never got that far, for the second ale, brewed with the utensils that I hadn't bothered to sterilize since leaving the ale to harden, quickly became slightly sour on its own. Even when taken in small doses it tasted foul. Well, beer is an acquired taste so I thought I would obviously have to persevere.

To cut a long and sour story short, I have to report that I never really enjoyed the sour beer, although I did begin not to notice its odd taste. I always ended up with violent and uncomfortable heart burn after about half a pint and so gave the exercise up and decided foxy beers were not for me. The price I paid for this experiment was high! I had always been a little cavalier about hygiene. After all, twenty years a brewer and never a sour one yet had led me to believe that you had to be criminally negligent to get a beer to go off. Not so! Having introduced the bacterium to my brewery it took me close to a year to brew another beer that didn't want to go sour at the drop of a King Keg. Be warned! Should an unwanted infection occur in your brewery then the addition of sodium metabisulphite to the young beer does help. Sulphur dioxide does not affect the yeast to any important amount but does give bacterial infections a hard time. The traditional method of adding ground eggshell, oyster shell etc. seems not to work at all. The idea was that these calcium carbonate containing items would neutralise the acid being produced by the vinous fermentation and then the drinker would not be able to taste it. If only it were true! Salt of Wormwood was also reputed to remove sourness, or hanging a bundle of hyssop in the beer. Unfortunately I've not been able to try either of these recommendations.

Another more likely method of rescuing a brew was to wait until the next brew was finished, keep back the draff and run the sour beer through this fresh draff. This method depends on the ability of malt grains to absorb the unwanted flavours. The beer should be heated to around 70°C (158°F) to kill the bacteria doing the damage, otherwise the beer will go off again within days. Distillers sometimes use a similar technique to get rid of the burnt flavour after a distillation.

They simply run the distillate through active charcoal powder, and that definitely works. Charcoal powder may leave the beer tasting of nothing though.

And talking of beers that traditionally never received a decent boil or amount of hops, and therefore should never clear before they have gone off, we cannot avoid taking another look at that old war horse Farrenbacher Weißbier. Eight minutes boiling time and still it clears. Twenty grams of hops and still it keeps. Go kick your mash tun you purists!

Porter.

No discourse on malt can be complete without mentioning Porter, that elusive beer that everyone has heard of but nobody drinks. It is important to know that for a beer so talked about but so little drunk, its introduction to the brewing public was as big a watershed in the history of brewing, as was the introduction of hops. Again it was economic pressures, which secured porter as the beer of the eighteenth century. Porter could be brewed in any weather; ale could not be brewed during the hottest months of the year in any quantity for the fermentation process is quite exothermic and large fermentation vats could only really lose the heat released by the fermentation, through the surface of the liquid. If the fermentation vat was covered to prevent the beer becoming foxed, less heat escaped and so the fermentation went faster and produced more heat. Ales regularly foamed out the fermentation vat. If the poor beleaguered brewer tried to get rid of the heat by rousing the beer, which was also common practice, he stirred in more air, encouraged infection and the aerobic fermentation, which releases twenty-five times as much heat as the alcoholic anaerobic fermentation. Furthermore most beer is drunk in hot weather at the very time one can't brew it. This regularly led to shortages, which could not be easily tolerated. For example, the Navy were most active in the summer months and often had to suffer sour beer on board. Imagine tying up in London in mid-July after months or maybe years at sea and finding no beer to drink in the whole town. The sailors were very reluctant members of the King's Navy anyway, and probably had been pressed into service by use of tricks, villainy and violence. The Admiralty knew it had to get beer for these men if uncomfortable and dangerous confrontations were to be avoided, and would commission breweries to brew no matter how ill advised the undertaking was.

Porter however, fermented more gently than ale and as such was more suited to large volume production in warm weather.

Mixtures.

One may think that it would have been difficult to find a market for a "new beer" and that the drinking public would reject porter, which was, after all, a beer of convenience to the trade, but it had at that time long been common practice to mix beers in the ale house. This was primarily done because many beers didn't keep well, so if one barrel needed using it would be mixed in the glass with a fresher sample in order to bring the hardened beer up to an acceptable taste. Some mixtures became popular and so would be ordered out of preference. A Brown Mixed is still common in Liverpool as is a Mild and Bitter in London. Porter was made popular to the drinker by claiming it had been brewed especially to imitate a frequently requested mixture and to that end a special porter malt had been kilned. The publicans were easy to win over too! It is certain that publicans found it a considerable nuisance to run to three barrels to mix one drink, (unless they had a poor quality beer to hide) and they were happy to introduce porter as a solution. So on all three fronts, brewer, publican and drinker, marketing porter was like running at an open door. The drink became so popular that in the sixty or so years after the introduction of porter by Ralph Harwood of the Bell Brewhouse in Shoreditch in 1722, many breweries referred to all sorts of mild, amber and brown ales as porter, probably in the hope of avoiding the leg-work involved in mixing an order, and to make the most of the popular demand this beer enjoyed. And this also explains the fact that later porters had everything but the kitchen sink thrown in. Odd- ball recipes containing peppers, capsicum, ginger and liquorice were common. Surely these were attempts to make a porter tasting beer without the hassle of making brown malt or running to three taps, and it also justifies the modern porter styles that are defined for competitions. All these things were porter to someone and all our modern day recreations surely have a historical precedent somewhere. Is there such a thing as a genuine "style"? Is Harwood's brown malt really essential?

Whatever! According to Mathias, Harwood's first porter was a "black thick beer, bitter to the tongue," of greater apparent strength and nourishment than existing ales. It required a malt dried and then kilned at a higher temperature than was usual for ales and was actually called Entire Butts by Harwood, meaning a mixture of half ale and half beer (half and half) or for the real connoisseurs a mixture of one third ale, one third beer and one third twopenny (a so called "pot of three threads" according to Bickerdyke).

Brown malt.

Many maltsters in Hertfordshire were already making brown malt and this is where the porter malt for London probably came from. Mathias indicates that Harwood's porter was perhaps a mixture of brown and amber malt although from Harwood's description it may have been predominantly from amber malt with some black malt. This would explain the slow fermentation, even in hot weather, for most of the extract from these malts would be caramelised starch and as such quite difficult for the yeast to break down. The alcohol content and therefore the rate of fermentation were perhaps regulated using paler malts and maybe sugar if that were allowed or the brewer could get away with it.

Now I doubt if there is a maltster anywhere making genuine brown malt as described by Stopes *(Historical Companion to House Brewing page 94)* and probably used by Harwood and so there isn't a genuine porter to be had anywhere, either from can or kit or public house. The closest one can get is Rauchmalz. It is extremely rare and to my knowledge Brupacks of Huddersfield are the only importers of this malt from its place of origin, Bamberg in Bavaria. The kilning of this malt is similar to that for brown malt and takes place over open fires using beechwood as the firing material. As the wood burns and volatilises, the aromas released permeate the malt and give it a smoky taste and flavour. It is expensive and although brown malt sounds like a tailor-made challenge for the House-Brewer, if I'm honest I have to admit that only the most dedicated among us can contemplate making it. So make yourself a Rauchbier using Brupacks recipe before you start and then you'll have a better idea of what your object malt looks like.

Brupacks Rauchbier.

Ingredients.

Rauchmalz (smoked Bavarian malt)	*4½ kg (9 lbs).*
Roasted Caramalt	*250g (½ lb).*
Northern Brewer hops (5.7% alpha-acid)	*45g (1½ oz).*
Wyeast 2206 or 2 sachets Gervin Lager yeast.	

Data. *The expected volume will be 22 litres (5 gallons) assuming a starting gravity of 1.048. A step mash decoction should be used, similar to that described on pages 118 and 119 of The Historical Companion, and later in this book.*

Fortified with your Rauchbier it is time to try a brown porter malt. Here goes!

Brown Malt for Porter.

The first problem to be dealt with is how to kiln the malt. Due to the process involved the malt takes up the quality of the firing material. In Hertfordshire in 1722 the most common fuel was coke but for a genuine brown malt, oak or beech faggots were used and the smoke was allowed access to the drying floor where it permeated the malt. Obviously an electric or gas fired oven won't really do if we're after the real thing. A wire mesh over a grill fired with beech is easy to achieve. But let's start at the beginning.

Making standard diastic pale malt.

The Steep *Sprinkle 2½ kg (5 lbs) brewer's barley on to the surface of 5 litres (1 gallon) of cold fresh water at around 8°C (46°F). Skim off any material which floats. Push a piece of plastic aquarium tube down through the grain and aerate the water with an aquarium pump. Maintain the temperature.*

Change the water after 4 hours and then twice daily until the barley has reached 40% water content. This will take around 72 hours, and should be done in the dark. The progress of the steep can best be followed by keeping tabs on the weight changes during the 72 hours it is in progress.

Barley is around 12% water. Therefore, the approximate dry weight of 2.5 kg of barley is:

2.5 kg - 12/100 x 2.5 = 2.3 kg

This 2.3 kg dry weight takes up water until it is 40% water or 60% barley. Its new mass is:

$$2.3\ kg/y \times 100 = 60\%$$

(y is the new mass of wet grain in kg).

$$y = 2.3\ kg \times 100/60$$

$$y = 3.83\ kg\ \text{wet barley.}$$

Some barley types may take up as much as 43.5% water, which yields a final steep mass of 3.9 kg.

Aim to be within this range.

A bucket with a perforated base (6mm) is invaluable for water changes.

Germinating	*A good steep may well advance the grain so much that the first roots are already showing by the end of the steep. The roots appear as tiny white "eyes" at the bottom of the grain. If these cannot be seen, then pour the wet grain into the perforated bucket, push it down into another bucket of the same size and holding a few centimetres of water, to give a good fit and pump air down the plastic tube going down through the grain and into the lower bucket. Weight the end with a piece of lead to hold it under the water. Wet air is now swept up through the grain and this keeps it damp. Keep this set up at just less than 16°C (61°F) until the "eyes" appear. Turn the grain twice daily to prevent heat build-up or root matting.*
Carbon Dioxide	*Suspend the perforated bucket and grain so that the carbon dioxide can freely pass out through the holes, but place a lid on the bucket to limit the amount of air that can be drawn through the top to replace it. The grain is thus kept in a carbon dioxide atmosphere. This encourages enzyme production but limits respiration and use of starch. Turn the grain as often as is needed to keep the grains separate and prevent heat build-up.*

By this time the weight of the green malt will have fallen to around 3.175 kg or 31% water.

Normal Drying — *Peel back the husk to reveal the growing shoot (acrospire). When this is two thirds the corn length, the green malt is ready to dry.*

Drying is normally done at less than 45°C (113°F) to protect the enzymes in this damp hydrolysing environment. The grain is spread thinly in a warm dark airy space, or in a fan assisted oven or an ordinary oven with the door open. Choose the lowest setting and make sure the temperature doesn't exceed 45°C (113°F). Normal drying may take as long as 2 days.

It is most useful if the grain is on specially constructed wire trays to allow maximum air circulation in the oven. I phoned around town with the help of the Yellow Pages (Wireworks or Wiremakers) and soon found some zinc covered steel mesh with 2mm^2 holes. I stapled the mesh to wooden frames made to fit my oven.

The drying phase is completed when the water content of the barley is nearly zero. The grain has also lost corn substance due to respiration and should now weigh 1.9 kg.

So 2.5 kg barley yields 1.9 kg of pale malt.

Kilning — *All malts are kilned for a few hours to give them their final degree of browning and texture.*

Brown malt isn't dried at all. The wet-green malt is immediately kilned by heating in the smoke and flame of a beech or oak faggot fire. This is best done on a small scale with the help of a charcoal grill or even better with a commercially available smoker. A wire tray must first be constructed to fit over the grill or smoker, through which the malt will not fall. Don't use your normal malt drying trays lest you set fire to the wooden frames.

Get a good blaze going in the grill or smoker and hold the malt just above the flames. It should not exceed 4cm (1½ inches) in depth. Turn the malt once to get an even texture. It wouldn't hurt to turn the malt more often but the technical difficulties of coping with turning and controlling the blaze meant that even professional 18th century maltsters didn't turn it more often.

All the water should be driven off in 1-2 hours. A moderate heat is maintained until nearly all the water is judged to have evaporated, and then the fire is stoked to produce a blaze. The sudden and intense heat causes the grain to swell by around 25% and the malt takes up the quality of the firing material. "Shot from a gun," as Quaker Oats call it.

High-class cabinet makers or fish smokers can help you get hold of some oak or beechwood chippings.

It is little wonder that brown malt fell quickly from favour. Eighteenth century reports indicate that there was considerable risk to the grain and then the malting itself catching fire, never mind the danger to the maltster. The latter was seldom considered in the brewing literature but he does get a mention in the brown malt making process. It must have been hazardous! Beware of modern malts which masquerade as brown malt. They are almost certainly Amber malt, which has been kilned a little more sharply.

Harwood's Original Porter.

We don't know Harwood's original porter recipe but the description of the beer leads me to believe it may have been something like this.

Ingredients.

Pale malt	*1 kg (2 lbs).*
Amber malt	*1 kg (2 lbs).*
Brown malt	*1 kg (2 lbs).*
Water	*5 litres (1 gallon) mainly calcium carbonate hard.*
Hops	*60g (2 oz) Northern Brewer.*
Sugar	*1 kg (2 lbs) molasses.*
Yeast	*1 sachet (7g) Muntons' dried top fermenting.*

Conditions.

1st mash	*Pour hot water onto the brown malt at 75°C (165°F). Stir in the pale and amber malts to settle the temperature out around 68°C (154°F). Mash for 1½ hours.*

2nd mash	*Run off the wort and mash again at 72°C (162°F)*
Sparge	*Sparge with 10 litres (2 gals) water.*
Boil	*Add the molasses and boil for 1½ hours with the hops. Cool quickly, strain and bring to a starting gravity of 1080. Ferment out at 20°C (68°F).*
Storage time	*6 weeks.*

Amber malt is now beginning to make a resurgence in the homebrew outlets and is an excellent starting point for stouts and mild ales. I've got into the habit of malting it myself as it was the easiest way to come by some, and of course it gives you several options the homebrew shop can't. A version of it is available from various suppliers but the problem is that "Amber" covers a variety of kilning temperatures, which until recently varied according to the preferences of the brewer and maltster. Brupacks amber does at least have some data with it and so one does actually know which Amber their malt is, but it cannot be the last word spoken on this malt. Here is a recipe for a very fine burnt stout, which turned out to be unique, which is the way beer used to be! Not only did I malt my own barley to make the beer but I also used hops, which were entirely home grown so I had to make up for the lack of bittering in my low alpha-acid Hallertauer by using heaps of them, but that's OK when you are picking more than you can use before next year's harvest. Of course Hallertauer wouldn't be a genuine stout choice, but historically brewers were never shy about using that which was available. I was also tickled by the prospect of making a beer almost entirely grown on my own dung heap.

Dunnington Double Burnt Stout.

I've named this stout after Dunnington Grange near the tiny Yorkshire village of Skipsea. It was here that I got a fine sample of lager barley, which the poor farmer was only too pleased to give away. Due to adverse weather during sowing, the barley had reached an unusable 13% protein, unusable that is for snooty brewers and maltsters who will try anything on to push prices down and not have to pay others for their toil. I asked for 10 lbs and received a bag nearly too heavy to lift. I think I could have had all 50 tons. The challenge was on to find a use for this barley and make a decent beer with it.

This is how I proceeded, determined to use nothing but home-grown ingredients. Of course I knew I could reduce the nitrogen content as a percentage of the malt substance by using a low nitrogen grist. In fact I used a zero nitrogen grist: granulated sugar.

Malting.

Steep	*4 kg (8 lbs) of high nitrogen pale lager malt (13% protein) was steeped 72 hours at 8°C (46°F). The water was aerated and changed daily. The wet barley weighed 7.2 kg (15 lbs) and was germinated at 12°C (54°F) until the acrospire reached two thirds of the length of the grain. This carbon dioxide bath was applied after 36 hours. The germination was completed in 6 days.*
Drying & kilning	*The green malt was dried for 18 hours at 35°C (95°F) to produce pale malt but some was finished for 6 hours at 120°C (248°F) to yield amber malt.* *200g (6½ oz) of green malt was quickly dried and kilned at 150°C (302°F) to make the black malt.*
Mashing	*2 kg (4 lbs) pale malt, 1 kg (2 lbs) amber malt and 200g (6½ oz) black malt were mashed in 4½ litres (1 gallon) carbonate hard water for 1½ hours at 72°C (162°F). The wort was run off and the draff mashed a second time with 2 litres (3 pints) water at 75°C (167°F) for 40 minutes.*
Sparge	*The wort was run off again, mixed with the first wort and the draff sparged with 4½ litres (1 gallon) water at 75°C (167°F).*
Boil	*10 litres (2½ gallons) extract were retrieved with a gravity of 1.062. 500g (1 lb) sugar were added to reduce the protein percentage and the wort was boiled for 1½ hours with 150g (5 oz) Hallertauer, which were added in equal portions at ½ hour intervals.*
Fermentation	*The wort was cooled quickly and diluted to 20 litres (4½ gallons) at 1.032. It was fermented out to 1.01 with a stout yeast at 18°C (64°F) and kegged with 90g (3 oz) lactose. This beer was tried at weekly intervals from the fourth week and was definitely at its best after 12 weeks.*

Beverley Brown Ale.

The same method was used to make an excellent brown ale with the following malt proportions:

Pale Malt	*2.8 kg (5 1/2 lbs)*
Amber Malt	*1 kg (2 lbs)*
Black Malt	*125g (4 oz)*

The pale malt was purchased but the others were made in my malting from the high nitrogen barley. I had intended to make a single stout but after a few glasses I changed the label and it definitely passed muster as a very fine brown ale. C'est la vie. The main thing is that it was a good beer and the speed it disappeared down my brother's throat after a night at the opera was commendation enough. Thirsty work is Verdi, even if we didn't sing a note.

The barley would have undoubtedly been rejected by a maltster but as I have already indicated, I got round the high nitrogen content by using some sugar and in so doing I reduced the percentage nitrogen in the soluble extract to a respectable level by adding a grit with no nitrogen in it. This is not allowed in Germany of course, where, since the Reinheitsgebot, one may not mash with anything but barley malt nor add any sugar. Smug brewers in the UK always believed that it was superior low nitrogen barley that enabled them to use the simpler infusion mash, and the high nitrogen low quality barley of the European Mainland that forced the continental brewer to use a decoction process to break up the heavy protein molecules. There may be something in this yarn. I can't judge. But certainly the legality of adding sugar to the wort or low nitrogen grits to the mash means that the UK brewer can artificially lower the proportion of nitrogen in the beer, and thus have a cheap and easy method of avoiding cloudy beers due to protein haze. It must be said here that my brown ale and double stout were superbly clear but because the original destination for the barley had been a lager, traditionally an all malt beer, my option was perhaps not open to the professional brewer! The point is though, that we should always stay flexible and work to our strengths, not to any dogma, for although many craft brewers shudder in horror at the idea of adding sugar to a wort, it does actually have a good pedigree. Throughout the eighteenth and nineteenth centuries common folk made ale from nothing but sugar, hops and yeast, for the unfair tax system on malt made it prohibitively expensive to obtain the malted grain. I quote from the anonymous *Art and Mystery.* The following précis describes the merits of brewing with sugar.

Sugar ale.

"Excellent ales may be brewed from sugar.

When we are denied the finest malts, what else are we to do but brew from sugar or from saccharine matter. The advantage is cost. 14 lbs of good refined sugar will produce an ale of equal strength as a bushel of malt. 16 lbs of Muscovado sugar will produce the same but with a deeper colour. Certainly the wholesome quality of the ale recommends itself since ales from sugar settle more lightly in the stomach. They are more easily digested, particularly if bottled. One needs fewer brewing utensils.

To make 20 gallons of good ale, boil the water with 3 lbs fresh hops for no longer than 10 minutes and pour it into a cask. The cask ought to be placed on end on a stillage. To the strained hopped liquor, add 28 lbs sugar totally dissolved at 70°F of heat. Strong fresh yeast must be stirred up among it. Fermentation will soon set in and cause the yeast to be forced out of the cork at the top of the barrel and being there confined in the rim of the chimb. It will chiefly run back again into the liquor and so again into the cask. In the usual warmth of our summers, it will require 3 weeks to a month to complete the working. After 10 days the cork should be firmly kept in the hole, yet removed every other day to admit air or to allow the fixed air to escape.

When the hissing noise has ceased the taste of the sugar will hardly be perceptible. The cork must only be firmly fixed in, in the week that the cask is to be tapped, about 2" from the bottom. The beer should be fine and bright and ready to be bottled."

John Richardson was a master brewer of the 1780s and while he often receives some derisory comments from later writers he obviously had a considerable impact on his contemporaries. Here is what he says of sugar ale, which he highly recommended although it sounds quite suspect.

John Richardson's 30 gallon Sugar Ale.

"Halve the hops (300g, 10 oz) and boil them in as little water as possible for five minutes. Add more water if necessary. Strain off hops and dissolve in 13 lbs sugar and a pint of good yeast. Pour the whole into a cask where fermentation will soon begin.

Stir every 2-3 days to give vent to the gases. When the fermentation is finished, the taste of sugar should be barely perceptible. Often people use scorched treacle or caramel. There is great purity of taste in this beer and it is easier on the stomach than malt ale. The whiter the sugar, so the lighter will be the ale.

It improves by age but is best kept bottled."

The other 10 oz of hops are not mentioned but maybe the beer was dry hopped with them for the practice was very common in Britain around that time. This would be an enormous amount kept back for dry hopping, bearing in mind that the present day copper hop to dry hop ratio would be nearer 10:1. It is likely that if they were used for dry hopping, they would be retained to copper hop the next brew.

More on Malt.

The availability of good malt has improved greatly over the last few years and due to this, the need to malt one's own barley has waned. As has been pointed out, only brown and amber malts are no longer easily available on the UK market and the only question mark over amber malt is that traditionally many malts kilned over a very wide range all went under the label "amber". To define which "amber malt" is being used, it is useful to look at the amount of colouring and extract that can be expected from that malt. Colour is usually measured in EBC units, although of course there are any number of other means of expressing this parameter. The lowest EBC rating is 2.5 and indicates the palest colour of a Pilsner malt. Black malt on the other hand can have a value of over 1000 EBU. The colour is measured by shining a light of a known intensity through a cell full of liquid and measuring the amount of light passing through. Traditionally the measurement was done by eye, comparing the colour of the test liquid with a colour chart. Nowadays the light intensity on the other side of the cell is measured electronically.

Secondly must be considered the diastic power of the malt. The more strongly the malt has been kilned, the more damaged the enzymes and the starch molecules will be. Consequently there will be less enzyme to break down the starch, but even if the dark malt is mashed with a pale malt to provide enzyme, the damaged partially caramelised starch molecules of the dark malt cannot be successfully broken down. The corn substance of such dark malts is largely lost to the fermentation and dark malts are consequently a considerable waste of money to the brewer. Before the hydrometer was invented brewers thought that a thick black wort had more extract in it than pale worts. Imagine the shock of using a hydrometer for the first time, spinning it into a wort as black as the night and watching it disappear beneath the waves! Even with this modern day wisdom on the subject I still find it a considerable shock to drop a hydrometer into gallons of black heavy wort and watch it sink nearly the whole length of its spindle.

A table of commonly available malts is included in Appendix 2.

Wheat malt.

The other malt of ever increasing importance is of course wheat malt. Wheat beers have shown a considerable resurgence over the last few years, despite the fact that they do not clear perfectly and they have a typical slightly sour taste. But their sudden popularity is evidence enough that drinkers are no longer so hung-up on insignificant issues such as clarity and are becoming more adventurous. Using wheat, oats or rye for malting was probably never a first choice historically but was determined by the harvest. Wheat is difficult to malt due to its lack of a husk to protect the acrospire.

The most famous and most enduring wheat beer of all time is Kölsch, which has remained on the market despite the lack of popularity of wheat beers for many years. As the name implies it is only brewed around the city of Cologne (Köln). Kölsch incidently, made legal history by being one of the first trademarks associated with a particular city, to receive protection.

It is top fermented (a rarity on the Continent) and not a pure wheat beer but a mixture of wheat and barley malt. Here is a recipe for Kölsch.

It should be drunk much colder than British top fermented beers.

Kölsch.

Ingredients.

Pilsner Malt	*3.5 kg (7 lbs).*
Light Munich or Pale Malt	*700g (1.4 lbs).*
Wheat Malt	*300g (0.6 lb).*
Perle Hops or Hallertauer (3% alpha-acid)	*100g (3 oz) for copper hopping.*
Tettnang or Hallertauer (3% alpha-acid)	*25g (1 oz) for dry hopping.*
Gervin top fermenting ale yeast	*1 sachet.*

Data. *Mash the grains as normal at around 64°C (147°F) and sparge. Boil the main copper hops for 1 hour and then ferment out at around 16-18°C. It may be better to use a lager yeast as they will certainly ferment out at around 6°C (61°F). If an ale top fermenter is used then it is better not to ferment out much below 18°C (64°F).*

Add the dry hops for the final two days of the fermentation. Keg or bottle the beer and lager for four weeks. Test the beer and drink cold when most palatable. It will probably not clear properly anyway and in Germany the yeast sediment is served with the bottled beer.

The finest wheat beer I've ever tasted was made by Dave Toner in his micro-brewery in Cabinteely, just outside Dublin.

Irish Wheat Beer.

Ingredients.

Wheat Malt	*3 kg (6¼ lbs).*
Lager Malt	*1 kg (2 lbs).*
Crystal Malt	*30g (1 oz).*
Irish Moss	*1 teaspoon.*
Hallertauer Hops	*50g (1⅔ oz).*
Wyeast	*3068*

Data. *22 litres (5 gallons) at SG 1.050.*

Mashing *The first thick mash is made from 11 litres water at 40°C (104°F), which is warmed with stirring to 50°C (122°F) and held for 30 minutes.*

This is then raised to 64°C (147°F) and maintained for 90 minutes, then raised to 71°C (160°F) to be held at that temperature for 20 minutes.

Finally the temperature is raised to 76°C (169°F) and held for a final 20 minutes. Whenever a mash is being heated, it must be constantly stirred. If there is obvious danger of burning, then thin the mash a little.

Sparging	*The draff is sparged with water at 78°C (172°F).*
Boil	*The hops are added to the combined wort and sparge water as soon as boiling has commenced. A vigorous boil is maintained for 2 hours, with the Irish Moss being added for the last 20 minutes.*
Fermentation	*2½ litres of hot wort is transferred to sterilised sealed bottles and stored cold for priming. The remainder is fermented at less than 22°C (72°F). 12 Hours after the vigorous fermentation has started, the froth is skimmed off. At the end of the primary fermentation the beer is racked into another container and isinglass added. It is then lagered for between 3-7 days at around 5°C (41°F).*
Conditioning	*Bottle or keg the beer using the priming wort proportionally. Keep at around 20°C (68°F) for 10 days to ferment out the primer and then for at least 5 weeks at 5°C (41°F). Serve at 9°C (48°F).*

Fast Wheat Beer.

Ingredients.	*As above but with the addition of 1 kg glucose.*
Mash	*The mash is warmed slowly and with stirring to 60°C (140°F) and held another 20 minutes.* *The temperature is finally brought up to 65°C (149°F) and held for 1½ hours.*
Sparging and boiling	*After sparging, the wort and sparges are boiled with the glucose and hops for 1½ hours. The Irish moss is added for the last 20 minutes.*

	The wort is cooled and brought to a starting gravity of 1050.
Fermentation	*The young beer is fermented out at 18°C (64°F) and bottled to be kept around 4 weeks before drinking.*

Irish moss is actually a seaweed, which when added to the boiling wort encourages the proteins to coagulate and helps the hot break. If a wheat beer is to be in any way clear, such adjuncts are probably useful.

Both these recipes are so-called step-mashes. This is a very traditional method of mashing by raising the temperature slowly from cold. There were obvious advantages to doing this in the days before brewers had thermometers at their disposal. Their methods of step mashing are still worth investigating.

Chapter seven.

Setting up your own House Brewery.

Parkes' Porter 1821.

"Boil $3^{1}/_{2}$ gallons of water and add a dash of cold to stop it boiling but too hot to hold the hand in.

Put in 1 peck of amber malt, enough to make it wet. Cover with a sack.

Mash $^{1}/_{2}$ hour.

Run out the wort and rerun it until clear. Use clean hay or straw as a sieve in front of the tap.

Mash again with $3^{1}/_{2}$ gallons for $^{1}/_{2}$ hour.

Immediately add a few hops to the worts to stop them turning sour.

Ladle fresh liquor over until the extraction is complete. Homebrewers add 1 lb treacle, some liquorice and Spanish liquorice.

$^{1}/_{4}$ lb hops is boiled with the first wort for 1 hour. Strain and boil in the second wort for 1 hour. Cool to 56-60°F, pitch yeast and cleanse after two days. Keep the casks filled. Replace overworkings with a bright beer, not with the overworkings. Avoid temperature changes which can excite a new fermentation. Put in some capsicum to warm on a winter morning."

Mashing the grain.

Many grain brewers, apart from those who are working on a professional basis, are, as in the wheat beer recipes, turning increasingly to the mash techniques practised in the eighteenth and nineteenth centuries although at a first glance I doubt that they recognise much of Parkes' brewing philosophy. Professional micro-brewers are using gravity feed to move the dry crushed grain into the traditional copper mash tun and using heavy duty slurry pumps to carry the wet draff from the mash tun to be sparged and then on to be disposed of. Such heavy duty machinery is beyond the scope and requirements of house-brewers but it is worth looking at the materials the professional chooses.

I assume that most non-professional house-brewers will find copper or stainless steel too expensive and I'm not convinced that we need to go for such high quality materials. In any case, we house-brewers will find it quite difficult to keep our equipment clean, especially the pipe-work, and we shall probably have to replace pipes regularly, at least every three or four years. Too large a capital investment is not reasonable for us. So although American and German homebrewers may well be spending over £1000 for their mash tun and a few pumps, I don't feel that I want to move into that league yet, especially as the rediscovery of the techniques of mashing at home is still very much in its infancy, and huge improvements may be expected in the next few years. All the while the market is developing so quickly it seems foolish to spend large amounts on equipment one may not wish to see as a long term investment. And isn't it much more fun to design your own House-Brewery? Here is a quote from an 1834 edition of a textbook on cottage and villa architecture. It is a description of a nineteenth century step-masher suitable for infusion mashes too and a design which can be copied in plastic and copper to fit into 6m^2 (45 sq. ft) of outhouse or shed. It contains much wisdom for a house-brewer contemplating buiding a brewery in preference to usurping the kitchen, and is the basis for the design I shall propose, although brick and wood will be replaced with polypropylene, the lift pump with an electric device, and the cooling trays with an immersible copper coil.

Loudon's house brewery.

"A very complete Brewery, on a smaller Scale, has been invented, and is now manufactured, by Messrs. Cottam and Hallen; of which fig. 1832 is the ground plan and fig. 1833 the elevation. In these figures: *a,* is the boiler, which holds one hundred gallons; *b,* the gallery for examining the boiler, and working the pump; *c,* the coolers, seven and a half inches deep; *d,* the mash tub; *e,* the cistern for receiving the wort from the mash-tub over it; *f,* the pump for drawing up the wort to be boiled; *g,* the cock by which the boiled wort is let into the coolers; h, a cock by which the hot water from the boiler is let down through the first cooler into the mash-tub upon the malt; and *i,* a cock and tube, by which the wort, when cooled, is returned to the mash-tub (after the grains have been removed from it), in order to be worked.

Remarks. The first brewery is one of the most complete things of the kind anywhere to be met with on a similar scale; and the second, not less so, on a smaller scale. The coolers, in the plan of Messrs. Cottam and Hallam, are of sheet iron and they are taken down and put up in very little time. The mash-tub, *d,* can also be removed so as to be out of the way when the brewhouse is used as a wash-house; and there is a cover to *e* for the same purpose. To save trouble, on first filling the boiler with water, it may be poured into *e,* and pumped up."
(Loudon 1833)

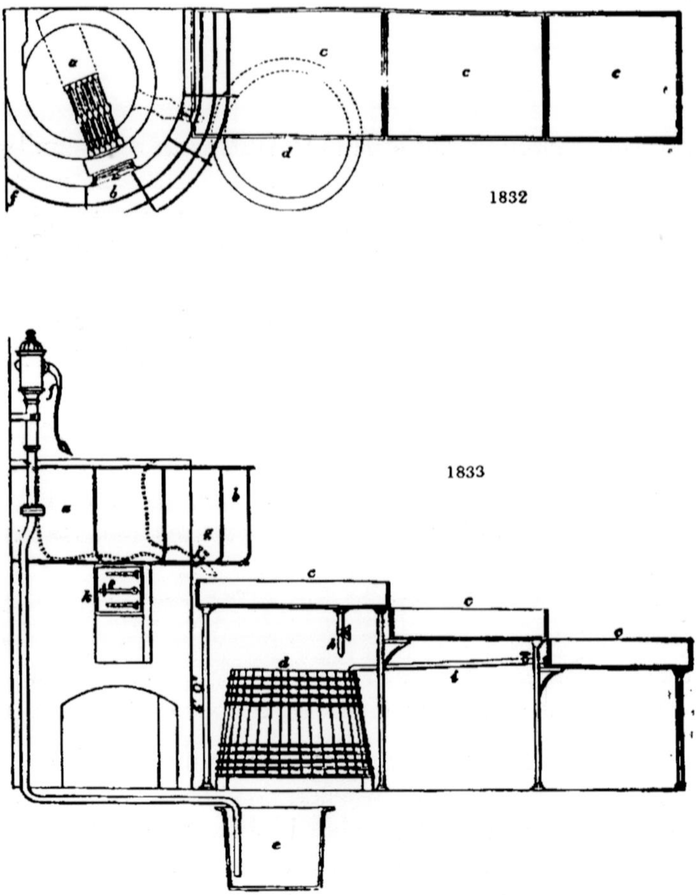

Plan and elevation of a small early 19th century domestic brewhouse.

In order to make a truly authentic beer of the period we would have to fly in the face of much modern wisdom. The use of flat-bed coolers allows air access to the hot wort, increasing the risk of infection and oxidation. I'm also sure that constructing parts of the brewery in sheet iron, which will quickly begin to corrode at such temperatures, must also affect the nature of the final product.

Nevertheless, it uses gravity to resolve many problems and allows a skilled operator exact temperature control on the grist by regulating the rate of circulation of the wort. Let us investigate the essential steps in creating a house-brewery.

Brewhouse suggestions.

The current mashing technique is to start with ready milled malt. Here we should be placing our very first question mark. In my experience homebrew wholesalers purchase malt that is ready crushed and as homebrewers are doubtless among their smallest customers, we get malt that is milled to someone elses specifications. Inevitably the malt is broken too long prior to sale. The homebrewer may reasonably store it for another month before he wishes to mash with it. Wrong milling size leads to all sorts of lautering problems throughout the mashing and sparging process whereas lengthy storage of crushed malt causes a loss in diastic power. I find that many grains are not broken at all while others are reduced to flour. The former prevents any significant diastic activity and makes maltose extraction quite impossible, while the latter floury substance not only slows water penetration of the grain but prevents run off of water during the sparge process. If the draff becomes waterlogged during sparging there is a real risk of the water running uselessly away down the walls of the sparge vessel or through a few channels it does find in the draff.

Huge amounts of maltose extract remain entrained in the draff because the water cannot be induced to flow through! Our mash efficiency drops to a fraction of what it should be and leads us into other sin and error, such as using too much sparge water in vain attempts to retrieve the situation and finally resorting to over use of sugar to counterbalance the maltose deficiency.

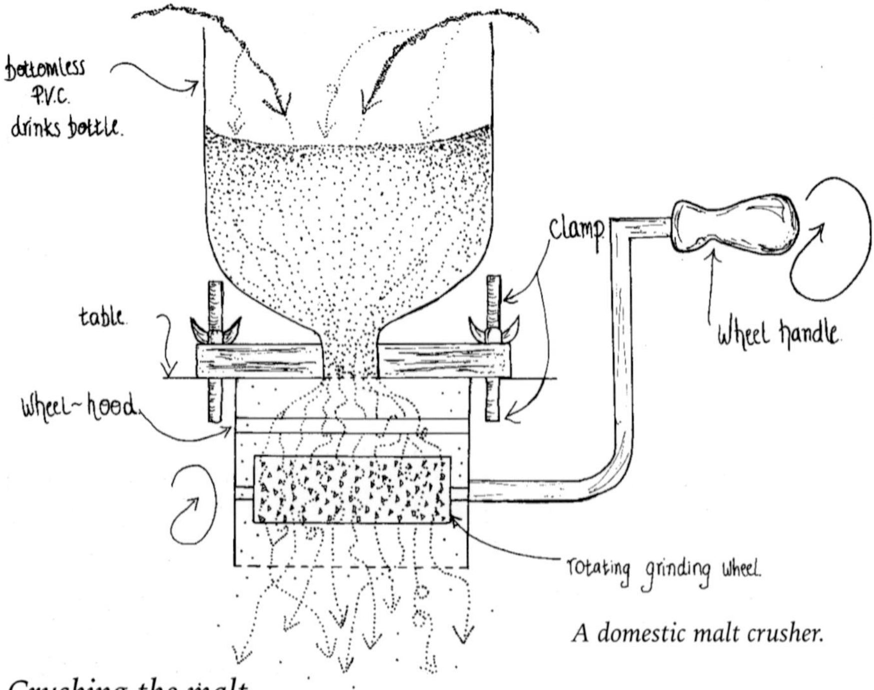

A domestic malt crusher.

Crushing the malt.

There is really no option but to purchase whole malt and grind it oneself or take it to someone who will grind it to our specifications, which would be the traditional and historically correct way to do it. Domestic malt grinders are expensive, most being imported from the United States, but they must take a top priority on our list of things to buy. Being realistic, we are unlikely to find any commercial miller prepared to grind our few pounds of malt to our specification and one should avoid milling too far ahead of brewing.

Whole malt grains keep their diastic power almost indefinitely assuming dry cool storage is available but once crushed, the malt immediately begins to deteriorate and shouldn't be stored in the crushed state more than four weeks. This is obviously another reason why we have to start crushing ourselves.

Homebrew shops obviously try to keep their stock turning as quickly as possible, but asking them not to keep malt longer than four weeks before it is mashed is quite unreasonable. Asking them to stock the uncrushed malt is not! There are also shops around which sell domestically produced grain grinders of about the right capacity for about one third of the imported price. Eventually, every enthusiastic house-brewer will start to malt the barley in order to gain total control over the whole process.

Not all malt will be perfectly friable and anything but a purpose built grinder is again going to leave us with all sorts of lautering problems.

Mash Temperature.

Our second major problem has always been accurate temperature control of the mash. The traditional eighteenth century answer to this problem was firstly to ignore it, but then, as one ever more realised the importance of the correct temperature, a wort circulating principle was used. To do this, the mash tun was divided into two parts.

The upper part is separated from the much smaller lower part by a lauter screen, which is nowadays a domed sheet of polypropylene perforated with hundreds of 3mm holes, but used to be simply a piece of straw or rush matting sitting on some wooden slats. The idea was that the wort could be easily drawn off from under the lauter screen with a ladle, heated to the correct temperature and returned to the mash tun by pouring it through the top to repeatedly run over the malt.

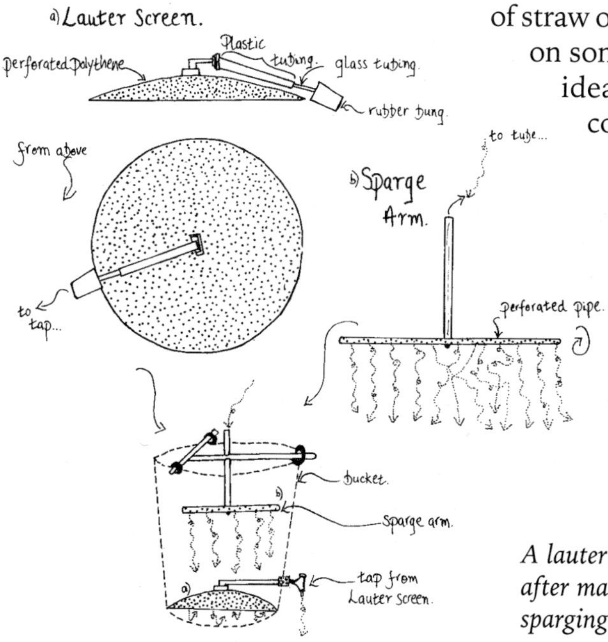

A lauter screen, still in place after mashing, for effective sparging using a rotary arm.

In earlier designs the perforated lauter bottom had a door in it and the whole mash tun was heated from below. The wort was ladled up through the door and poured back onto the malt, but in later versions, the lauter bottoms had a pipe fitted to them so that the wort could run off through a tap, be heated externally and then returned to the mash tun when it was at the correct temperature.

This method still allows us easy mechanisation. A small pump can be used to circulate the wort from the bottom of the mash tun (under the screen) up into a temperature regulated electric boiler and then we can gravity feed this gently back into the top of the mash tun. The beauty of this circulating wort procedure is that the wort is sparging the grains all the while, becoming ever more concentrated in extract and at exactly the right temperature when it hits the grains. When the mash is finished, the wort is directed into a third vessel for holding, and replaced in the circulation by hot water, the head of which is sufficient to drive a spray mechanism. This sparge water is finally run back into with the wort container, pumped back to the boiler and boiled with the hops. Another elegance of this very traditional method is not immediately evident but of vital importance. The circulating wort inevitably carries particles of size less than 3mm, through the lauter screen. Eventually the screen becomes covered in particles greater than 3mm in size and these then form a bed of draff capable of collecting particles of slightly smaller size than they are. This principle repeats itself until even the tiniest particles are trapped on the lauter screen and perfectly clear wort is circulating.

The wort and sparges can then be lifted to the boiler for boiling with the hops and then gravity fed to the fermenter through a coarse filter placed in the boiler outlet to catch any hop flowers, which may be carried down with the wort when it has finished boiling.

Hahn and Historical Brewing.

My first evidence of this technique being recorded was by Johann Gottfried Hahn in 1804 and Parkes in 1815 but these may not be the originators of this method. In fact Hahn found the idea in some papers of the father of an unnamed friend, so the method could be anything up to fifty years older. It was certainly the recommended procedure for all house breweries by 1833, as can be seen from Loudon's recommended design of a nineteenth century domestic brewhouse. Nevertheless, it seems appropriate to give Hahn the credit and provide some recipes which he and Parkes used.

Bohemian Hausbier by J. H. Hahn.

Hahn's mash tun was 5 foot across and 3 foot high. This gave it a capacity of around 29 gallons or 140 litres. It was heated directly by the flue gases of a fire beneath the tun. The malt was held above the hot wort by a lauter sieve made of wood slats and covered with straw or some type of rush matting. Over the straw was laid a piece of finely woven linen. This mat is important for if fresh straw were used for every brew, this gave the beer a very original and characteristic flavour (cf. Parkes' 1821 Porter). I'm sure that adventurous house-brewers in the past have brewed some very interesting beers by covering their lauter bottom with fresh straw. It was in fact common in the Middle Ages to flavour and fine beer with fresh straw.

Brewing Machines.

Hahn describes his process as follows:

> The lauter bottom *(L)* had a trapdoor *(S)* fitted through which the wort could be lifted and poured through the mash. The base of the tun *(fig.3)*, which is in contact with the flue gases was made from copper sheet *(Q)*, firmly nailed to the wooden rim which couldn't come in contact with the fire.
>
> The volume L *(fig. 2)* was filled with good clean soft spring water and the broken malt poured onto the lauter bottom M. The fire was lit *(G)* and water heated until one couldn't hold one's hand in it.
>
> (This is usually around 60°C (140°F) although a hardened brewer may have been able to withstand temperatures a little above this).
>
> The water was lifted with the help of a ladle through the trapdoor *(S)* and poured through the malt. This was continued until the wort reached the boil.

This may have taken several hours if 100 litres (22 gallons) of water were being heated and so the wort probably reached the hot break during this time. Furthermore, the continual filtration through the straw mat removed any solids during the mash.

As soon as boiling point was reached, the fire was put out and the wort run out the tap *(B)* into a fermenter *(D)*.

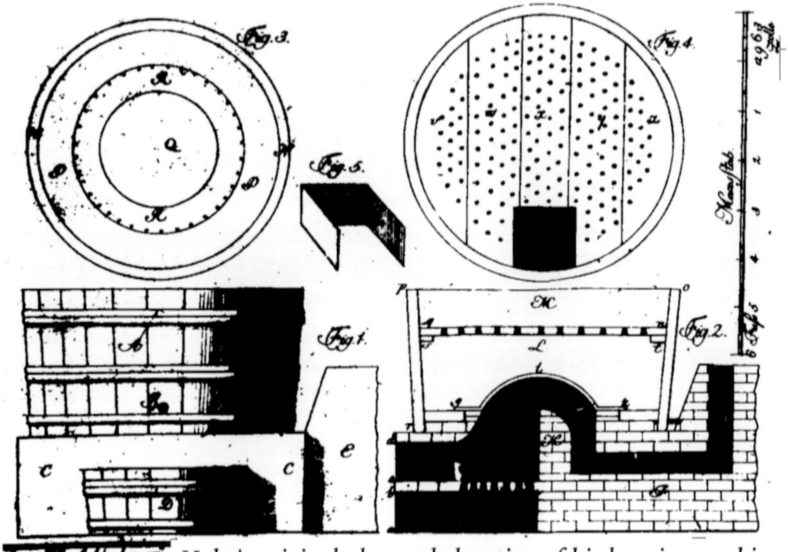

Hahn's original plan and elevation of his brewing machine.

Hahn didn't sparge the draff. He either mashed a second time and combined the two worts or used the second wort for brewing a lower grade thinner beer, often called "table beers" in Britain at that time.

Making table beers was not considered in any way a waste or something to be scorned for people drank beers at all times of the day and night, instead of using water which more often than not carried infectious diseases. Obviously they didn't always want a high alcohol beer and were quite glad to use the second worts for brewing a breakfast beer.

The stronger the wort, the less power it has on the hops but the finer will be the quality extracted.
(18th century brewer's aphorism)

And now for the second big Hahn surprise! We've had the straw to impart flavour. What about the hops. Hahn insists that it was not common practice in South East Germany and Bohemia to boil the hops with the wort. Although he admits that many brewers did just that, he found the sugar and protein extract in the wort to be most detrimental to the extraction of hop flavours. Our brewer's aphorism had crossed international boundaries.

He gave no rational reason as to why the dissolved solids in a wort should affect the extraction of hop flavours, so it is fair to assume that the real reason for this inconvenient practice was one of taste. Presumably by not boiling the hops with the wort, he could achieve a quite different flavour and texture in the beer, which was apparently a nuance he preferred. This is obviously a direction which the enthusiastic house-brewer may wish to investigate so here is Hahn's preferred option, which he quotes as the way the Bohemian brewers of the late eighteenth century hopped their beer. Some of the finest beers are still brewed in Bohemia including Urquell which I shall come back to later. Here is the Bohemian method of extracting hops as recorded in 1803 by Möller of Osnabrück.

Suit the colour of the hops to the colour of the beer. Brown hops for brown beer. Pale hops for pale beer. Ripe hops are brownest. (18th century brewer's aphorism).

How simple early brewers had it. I doubt many craft brewers nowadays would appreciate the perfect fool in that statement. And yet it probably served them well for centuries. Even Hahn was more adventurous than that!

Hop Extracts 1803.

> "One takes 44 litres (10 gallons) of best garden hops, 1/2 cup of juniper berries, 3/4 cup of salt, and 1 lb of kaolin. All this is boiled with some wort from a thin beer until the hops retain no flavour. The liquor is strained through a muslin bag and thoroughly wrung out and then the clear extract cooked so long until it shows signs of forming a jelly. This thick goo is then left to dry in a shady but draughty spot and kept until needed."

It is difficult to see the logic in this process. The boiling will remove all the aromatic oils and isomerise the alpha-acids. One might presume the Bohemians liked their beer very bitter but as they tend to use many low alpha-acid hops such as Saaz, this doesn't seem a sensible explanation of the practice. It could be that the hassle of drying and storing a huge volume of hop flowers in a hot country with frequent high humidity thundery weather was too complicated, never mind the problems of rats and mice in the store, but this argument can only be partly true for the extracting process is hardly convenient. I think we have to look for the taste flavours, rendered by the juniper, salt and hops and the effect the kaolin had on these flavours to find the real reason for this preferred method of separately extracting hop oils. Juniper has long found uses in gin and Schnapps preparation and gives its name to the Dutch Schnapps called Genever. It is hardly surprising that it was at some time or another used in beer. The salt Hahn claims encouraged the yeast to settle out quickly while the kaolin preserved the beer in the summer months and prevents sourness. Maybe but I doubt it. If salt encourages yeast to settle out quickly then it is because salt discourages yeast activity. I think he just preferred the taste of beer made with hops, juniper, salt and kaolin and because he was trying to put brewing on some kind of scientific basis, thought he ought to have a good explanation for a thoroughly odd process.

We should however be grateful to him as it gives us another route to try in our attempts to get a greater variety of beers.

Or is Hahn's method so odd? Many modern brewers use pre-isomerised hop extracts for flavouring. I had always assumed this to be for the sake of convenience, but it seems to have a historical pedigree.

Aromatic extracts.

"Others extracted hops by soaking the flowers in cold water for several hours (which will take out some of the aromatic oils) and then boiling the hops in a little water until they have lost all their taste and the water has become quite brown. Wringing the flowers out in a muslin cloth and leaving the extracts (the cold and the hot) in shallow trays until they have evaporated to a thick jelly was common. This is then gently warmed to dryness and the powder stored dry. Six Loth (84g, 3 oz) of this extract is the equivalent to 450g (1 lb) of hop flowers."

Here we have a method of preserving the aromatic oils by first leaching them out in the cold water.

Equally as interesting is this description from *The Art and Mystery of making Ales & Beers*. London 1865.

"Tincture of Hops.

1) Take 12 oz fresh hops and steep them in a pint of proof spirit.
2) Let it digest for 20 days.
3) Strain to filter and bottle and add it to weak worts in warm weather. It has a narcotic effect like opium but not so disastrous."

We are short on detail here and it certainly sounds like an experiment that needs to be done with care.

When boiling hops, do take care to reflux as much of the steam issuing from the saucepan during the boiling phase, back into the saucepan. A large dead volume above the liquid is useful and cool the lid with a damp cloth.

Back to Hahn's beer. This is what he has to say on the subject of fermentations.

Fermentations.

> "Put as much of the extract into the tub (D) as is apposite and then pitch a good yeast."

Hahn's yeast came from a previous brew and was a strong working top fermenter. Within a few hours of the yeast being pitched the surface of the young beer was covered in a thick foam.

As soon as the brewer judged this first phase to be completed, the swimming yeast was carefully removed and the beer was filled into casks right up to the tap hole in the top. This idea of racking for the first time just prior to the yeast head sinking, finds several references in English brewing literature. The secondary fermentation doubtless led to spillages. The barrels were kept full by topping up with some wort kept back for the purpose.

In summer Hahn cooled the fermenting wort to 15°C (59°F), in autumn and spring to 17.5°C (64°F) and in coldest winter to 25°C (77°F). These temperatures were decided upon bearing in mind that fermentation is an exothermic process, (cf. Harwood's Porter) and the rate of heat loss from the fermentation vat had to compensate for the heat production during the fermentation. Further temperature regulation was achieved by covering or uncovering the vat but in any case the primary fermentation, during which time the yeast used all the available oxygen for reproduction of yeast cells, had to be finished within 6 hours. Longer than this was considered very detrimental to the beer.

In order to be able to brew historical ales and beers, it is essential to be able to manage one's own yeast. Here is an English description from around the same time and then we'll look at some emulation techniques.

> "A space of 2 days and nights is needed, then the fermentation will naturally abate and by degrees cease. This can be satisfactorily ascertained by the falling of the head through the wort which shows that fermentation is declining. Then the wort must be drawn off into casks. Beer should be drawn carefully and gently. Keep the casks quite full.
>
> The second fermentation may cause running over, so the casks should be topped up 2 or three times a day with wort kept back for that purpose. Once fermentation has ceased, close the casks up and keep them till the beginning of the year following, (assuming one brews in October)."
>
> *Art and Mystery of Brewing.*

Getting a Grip on Yeast.

Present day Home and House-Brewers can be broadly divided into two camps. In the first and most populace group are those who open a packet of dried yeast, throw it into their unfermented wort and don't spare a single thought about what happens next in their fermentation. And then there are those who talk of nothing else than their yeast strain and how they nurture it and the effect it will have on their brew.

Yeast belongs to the group of micro-organisms which the bio-technologists would call fungi or we would call mould. They don't look as though they have much to do with mushrooms or fungus and you'll be pleased to know that when viewed under a microscope yeast cells look nothing like the mycel shaped threads of other nasty moulds we are familiar with. In fact within limits these little spheres, a mere 0.02mm diameter, should be present in the naturally occurring gut flora in our body. There can be little danger then in drinking beer or wine containing these invisible loners, unless you are suffering from one of those nasty complaints connected with a yeast overgrowth such as thrush or candida albicans. These are very unpleasant illnesses although not in that sense dangerous. So if starchy or sweet foods or home made beers make you feel ill or flatulent, go and tell your doctor.

And there we have a key feature of yeasts; they use starch and sugar molecules as their energy supply (just as we do) and provided there is enough oxygen present they multiply very quickly by growing a bulge, which eventually splits off as a new cell. This process releases carbon dioxide, water, baby yeast cells and much energy, but no alcohol! It is of course the process loved by the baker and that is why he kneads his dough to get plenty of air in it to make sure he gets aerobic fermentation, for the carbon dioxide so produced makes the dough rise.

Many brewers rouse their worts prior to fermentation. Some aerate the hot wort which radically alters the flavour and colour of beer due to wort oxidation. The argument for this hot wort aeration seems to be that any infection is eliminated at such temperatures. Others aerate the cold wort which causes no obvious change to the beer but can introduce infection.

But in the absence of oxygen, unlike many organisms, which die, the yeast cell simply changes course, stops multiplying, and instead of making water and carbon dioxide, we get alcohol and carbon dioxide. This then is the process the brewer and vintner prefer. As it releases about one twentieth the energy of the baker's process we have to keep our fermentations at the right temperature.

Unfortunately yeasts aren't the only microbes that can use sugar as an energy source but most of the others do not turn it to alcohol. Other fungi and bacteria can produce an evil mixture of compounds as well as occasionally some alcohol, but we can shut them out of the equation with a little care.

1) Yeasts like things gently acidic, bacteria don't! Our worts should naturally end up at pH 4-5 during and after mashing, and this is acidic enough to give the yeast a flying start in the fermentation race at the expense of any unwanted bacteria.

2) Other fungi will not be able to compete with a good brewer's yeast because our clean working and sterilised fermentation vat means that the wild yeasts can only be present in low concentrations. By the time they have multiplied enough to affect our beer, the brewer's yeast we've added has done the work. This is enhanced by the fact that all fungi have the knack of creating the conditions under which they work best, so the first to get going, inevitably wins the race.

So once one knows how yeast works, it is but a matter of common sense to give our brewer's yeast exactly what it wants. Here are some more do's and don'ts.

3) Never dilute your wort prior to fermentation with water from the hot water system. Only good honest cold water is saturated with oxygen and in the first phase we want aerobic fermentation so that the yeast can multiply. A good supply of dissolved oxygen is essential.

   Some brewers aerate the wort with an aquarium pump. It is a good idea to filter or sterilise the air before it enters the wort.

4) Keep a fermentation well covered to keep out additional air. Once the yeast has used all the dissolved oxygen in the unfermented beer we want it to continue to ferment anaerobically (no oxygen) so that it makes less carbon dioxide and more alcohol. After the initial phase, aerobic fermentation is a waste of sugar. However, a good blanket of carbon dioxide in the vat gives many bacteria a hard time because by now we should have eliminated the ones that want to work anaerobically, during the first (aerobic) phase. If we now switch to predominantly anaerobic fermentation, we can stitch up the ones that are left. Neat? Or what? So don't keep opening and shutting a fermentation. It's important not to change the atmosphere once started.

Having said that, many old-time and quite a few modern micro-breweries still use open fermentation vats and rely on the fact that carbon dioxide is heavier than air and the wort is covered in a thick mat of yeasty bubbles, to prevent too much air getting at the fermentation. Such brewers do work under fairly ideal temperature and hygiene conditions and although I'm the first to go for authenticity, I do still cover my vat.

5) We should always make up a good working starter well before we anticipate pitching the yeast. This makes sure the brewer's yeast wins the concentration stakes at the expense of any wild yeasts or bacteria, which can't get a good foot in the door.

Yeast starters are especially important when using dried yeasts from a sachet as the yeast cells have been dehydrated and have to absorb water before they can become active again. The high concentration of sugar in a wort seems to slow the osmotic up-take of the essential water. To hydrate a dried yeast, follow this procedure.

Dried Starters.

1) Procure an Erlenmeyer or other narrow necked flat bottomed flask with a good fitting airlock. $^1/_3$ fill both with water and place

Variations of yeast cell concentration and SG with days after pitching

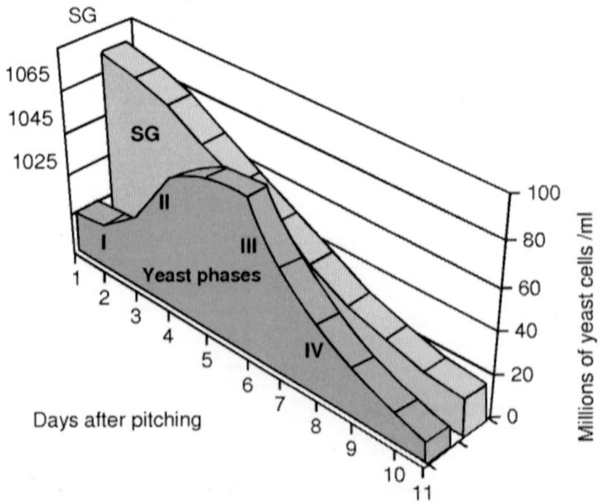

them in a microwave on maximum power for 1 minute. Steam should be issuing from both.

2) Allow the water to cool to 36°C (97°F) and add the sachet of dried yeast. After 10 minutes the cells should be hydrated enough to be added to a sample of aerated wort to make up a proper starter.

This procedure ensures a higher concentration of viable cells go into the starter.

Use of the microwave for sterilising does do long term damage to rubber bungs and plastic air-locks but they are cheap enough. There is however no quicker way to sterilise small equipment and pressure cooking for up to 30 minutes, which is the microbiologist recommended method, does much more damage to plastic and rubber.

It is important to note that the very first lag, or initial phase of a yeast starting work, during which time the yeast absorbs nitrogen, sugars and oxygen, does not need to take place when using a full working yeast sample. If however your starter is from a dried yeast or culture then this phase has to be completed before fermentation proper can start. The lag phase (I) will take around 8-12 hours at 7-10°C (45-50°F), or half this time for top fermenting ales at 18-20°C (65-68°F).

If the cells first need to take up nitrogen containing compounds, sugar and oxygen, a straight sugar solution as a starter cannot supply the nitrogen compounds and is no good. Only wort will do!

At this stage in starting our yeast we should be as much as a day away from having some wort available, unless we had the foresight to save a little from our last brew.

Saving a wort (microwave).

1) Take an old screw top baby food bottle or similar and $^{2}/_{3}$ fill it with wort. Cover it with film and microwave it and its plastic lid (containing some water) for 5 minutes starting at full power. It should start boiling within 3 minutes, when the power must be lowered to prevent the wort boiling over. Take care not to use metal tops in the microwave.
2) Screw the top down firmly and store in the fridge until needed. Use oven gloves.

(Pressure cooker).

1) Boil the wort to get the air out, fill the bottles and screw down or cap. Give the wort the works in the pressure cooker for fifteen minutes. Store it in the fridge until needed, (not longer than six months). Take care not to use plastic tops in the pressure cooker.
2) So before you start mashing, take the yeast preparation, hydrate it if it is a dried yeast and then swirl it into the sterile wort from a previous brew. This is now your starter.
3) As soon as the yeast and wort are ready for pitching, stir the starter into the main wort and cover. The respiration phase (II) now starts. The dissolved oxygen is used by the cells for reproduction. There is still no marked reduction in the specific gravity of the wort but carbon dioxide gas should be evident. There is little alcohol production but a significant drop in pH to around 4. This respiration phase lasts around 6-8 hours for

warmly kept top fermented beers but is significantly slower for cool bottom fermenters (12-16 hours).

Once established, i.e. the respiration phase is completed, a good fermentation looks rocky, like a moon landscape, full of weird and wonderful shapes growing up out of the wort. After a few days, as the density of the fermenting beer decreases, this yeast blanket sinks. Before it does so is the time to carefully scoop off any brown resinous material which floats on the yeast blanket. Take care not to expose the surface of the beer. It is during this phase (III on the graph) that the specific gravity drops most quickly and should start about one day after pitching a working yeast.

Many dried yeast users find that phase III can take anything up to four days to start and this is almost certainly the effect of maltreating the dried yeast as it comes out the sachet, or failing to get enough oxygen in the wort.

The final phase IV occurs when the density of the wort has decreased sufficiently for the yeast to start to sink. The yeast particles are becoming larger during phase III as the carbon dioxide production reaches such a rate that it swirls the yeast and the multitude of other suspended solids present around in the vat, causing collisions, coagulation and finally precipitation.

Yeast flavours.

The exact strain of yeast also affects the flavour of the beer. Such flavours depend on the ability of the yeast to produce or suppress the production of esters, which have a typically fruity smell and flavour; diacetyl, which is typified in butterscotch, and 2,3-pentadione which puts us in mind of honey. These, and many other compounds such as the fusel oils, should only be present in such minute quantities that an exact identification with the palate is often impossible. Experienced beer judges and brewmasters however seem to be able to pick out these flavours with complete reliability. I manage to enjoy them without being able to identify or talk about them.

Top and Bottom Fermenters.

Your homebrew stockist will offer you two basic types of yeast. The most widely used are so called top fermenting yeasts and these tend to be less dense than bottom fermenters so they swim on the surface or stay suspended in the wort longer. They need temperatures above 16°C. As they are likely to have longer access to the air, and don't produce as much alcohol, i.e. waste more sugar making carbon dioxide, they do not tend to reach the same degree of attenuation as the bottom fermenters. This isn't really a problem on the scale we work on. Bottom fermenters however sink soon after pitching and work at much lower temperatures. This gives a purer fermentation.

There is probably little real difference between these two yeast types but just as no two people are identical, so we may suppose are no two yeast cells. Some sink, some float, some like it hot, others prefer it cool. By controlling the fermentation conditions and propagating the yeast cells that survive best under those conditions, we can develop our own house strain and propagate it to keep for future brews. The longer we work with a particular strain under the same conditions, the more we weed out the cells that don't flourish under those working conditions. This is how we achieve and propagate our particular strain of yeast for our very own house brew.

Professional brewers never use dried yeast cultures. They purchase their yeast in liquid suspension or on micro-biological plates and propagate it. Some large breweries never need purchase yeast as they always produce more than they need and by careful management can maintain that strain in first class condition. It becomes a trade secret. They do however employ a specialist laboratory to look after a sample of their yeast and propagate it in case the worst brewing calamity possible occurs and they infect their culture. Small breweries use a strain for two or three brews and then as it begins to weaken they purchase another sample from the professional laboratory and re-grow their culture. This saves them the labour of taking care of their yeast strain. There is no reason why we should not do the same!

Using a liquid yeast culture?

The first advantage is that you can develop your own unique house brew for there is nothing to stop you keeping your own liquid culture. The liquid cultures you buy are totally pure, and may even have been developed from a single yeast cell, although I can't promise this. No wild yeasts means no wild flavours. You are in complete control! You should also be able to obtain a more consistent brew if that is important. I often get asked why I don't brew another beer like the last time. The answer is "I can't," well not with sachet yeasts. This doesn't trouble me, but if it's a problem for you, try a culture.

So why aren't we all using liquid cultures of our favourite strains? They work out expensive unless you start propagating your own culture. Furthermore it's a messy business to re-culture and assuming all these problems are out the way, you will still need to make a yeast starter from your last wort, about a week before the next brew. If you forget to do this, I'm afraid it's come back sachets, all is forgiven! If you're not interested in propagating, simply buy a bottle of liquid culture and follow the instructions! It's an expensive option though.

So having established that starting and propagating a yeast culture is not for the faint hearted, the next step is getting the gear. If looking the part is important to you when brewing, consult the Yellow Pages under Medical Suppliers, Biology Suppliers or School Suppliers. Any such company should be able to sell you McCartney bottles for very little. These are little screw top bottles with a rubber seal to take a hypodermic needle, and then reseal as the needle is withdrawn. That way the contents stay sterile much longer. Tell the supplier what you want them for, that you are a home brewer propagating a yeast culture, and they won't mind selling you a few 20ml hypodermic syringes as well. A pressure cooker is useful but don't bother to rush out and buy one. Sterilising in boiling water works too but you must boil the equipment for at least 1 hour to let the high temperatures get right through into any nooks and crannies. Even then I wouldn't try to keep the worts indefinitely if you don't have a pressure cooker. With a pressure cooker we can talk months. Microwaving or boiling water should allow the worts to be kept several weeks.

Yeast starters from a culture.

We have two variations of the same method. Here's the first, as reported by the Australian home brewer Murray Young recorded in *Ausbeer No. 3.*

1) Half fill a McCartney bottle with wort and gelatine. 1/2 teaspoon gelatine in a 25ml McCartney is plenty.
2) Screw down the tops with the rubber septum in place and pressure cook for 15 minutes.
3) When cold, take the liquid culture according to the manufacturers recommendation and inject some through the septum, into the sterile wort/gelatine mixture.
4) Loosen the cap slightly to allow air to escape. A day later you should see a yeast head forming. Put them in the fridge until needed.

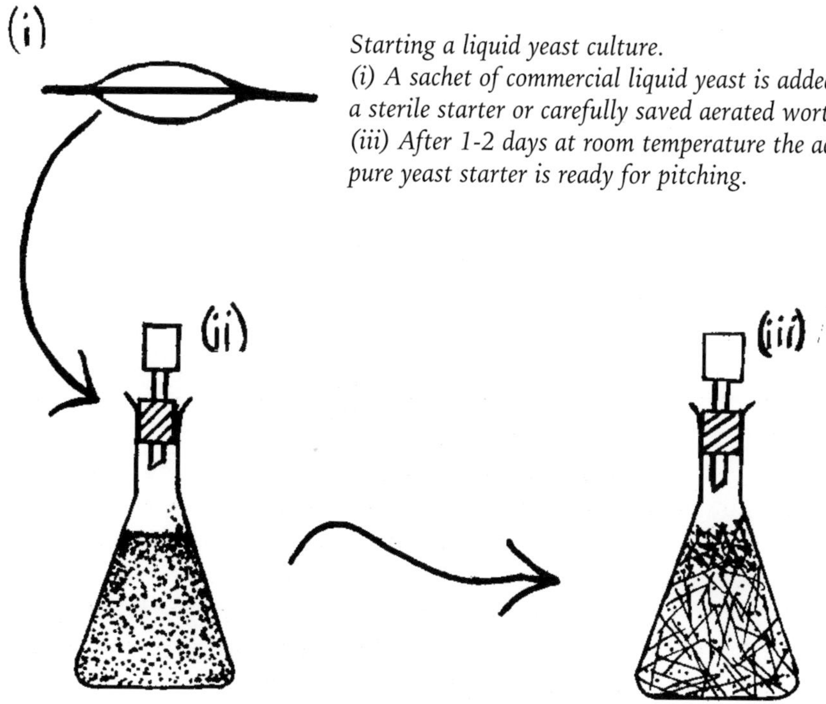

Starting a liquid yeast culture.
(i) A sachet of commercial liquid yeast is added to a sterile starter or carefully saved aerated wort (ii)
(iii) After 1-2 days at room temperature the active pure yeast starter is ready for pitching.

Irish method.

Far simpler and probably as effective is the method shown me on a visit to Ireland by Dave Toner, who sterilises all his glassware in the microwave.

1) ¼ fill screw top stubbies etc. with water and microwave on high for 2 minutes. Instead of water one can use wort and then the jar and wort are sterilised in one procedure. Fish the screw tops out of boiling water and seal immediately while everything is still piping hot. Don't forget the oven gloves!
2) To propagate the culture, take a small sample as recommended by the manufacturers and put it into a well boiled out (or microwaved) milk bottle with the sterile wort and a crystal of yeast nutrient.
3) Fit an airlock, which has been boiled for 1 hour or microwaved for 2 minutes and containing sterilising solution. Take care not to overfill the airlock or a drop in temperature can cause the solution to suck back into the yeast/wort. Keep this at 20°C (68°F) until a good fermentation is evident. This is then ready for pitching.

Dave has kept a genuine Guinness culture going for years by starting it in this way and propagating it.

Your new mash is nearing completion. You've got it on to boil. Well it's too late to use your culture this time!!! Take out a sachet.

Four days ago you should have taken a sterile wort, taken the top off, held the opening over a gas flame for a few seconds, and then injected 15ml of your yeast culture. Cap the stubby glass bottle with an airlock if you can get one to fit, or with cotton wool otherwise, and keep it between 16-20°C (60-68°F). Remember! Working near a gas flame means that a constant stream of sterile air is wafting around you. Not a bad idea.

After 2 days, mix the contents with another 4 sterile worts and 2 days later it's ready to pitch. That way you increase four fold the actual concentration of yeast cells going into the wort. But you must think ahead!

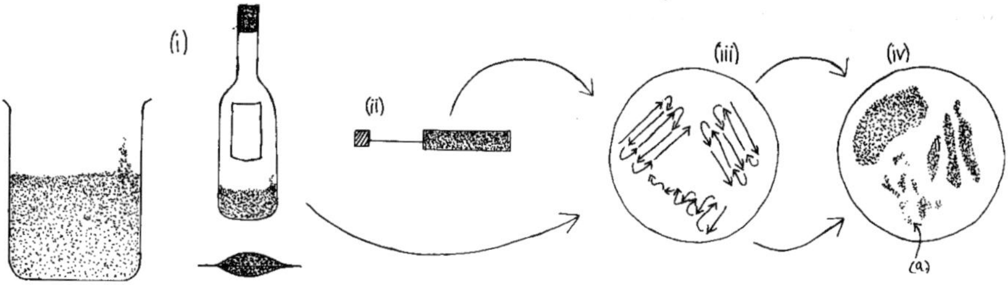

Active yeast slurry from a previous brew (i) is carried across with a sterile wire loop (ii) onto a petri-dish of malt agar (iii). After steady incubation over 4-5 days colonies begin to grow (iv). If you buy a slant, this work is done for you and the growing takes place in the post.

Propagating Yeast.

Any house-brewer who takes himself seriously will want to propagate yeast. You'll know there is no magic to mashing a fantastic beer. You get good ones because you apply old-fashioned common sense and you empathize with your medium. Unless you can do this, and not everyone can, the best ingredients in the world won't brew you a first rate beer. But having got a brew, which takes your breath away with its excellence, you'll want to know how to repeat exactly that beer. Well it probably isn't possible. It is impossible to repeat the conditions applied to one brew on subsequent mashings, and if you use a different yeast every time, then you will always achieve a different beer. However if we propagate a yeast, i.e. save a yeast from one brew for the next, we will always take a yeast of known good characteristics for our particular kind of beer and pass on its qualities to the next brewing and we may get closer to a standard house brew.

When to collect a yeast.

I have dealt with the two distinct fermentation phases, aerobic (with oxygen) and anaerobic (without oxygen), and we agreed that during the first aerobic phase, the yeast is using sugar and oxygen to multiply but is producing little or no alcohol. During this time, the yeast is building a foam blanket on the surface of the wort, and so we don't want to use this foam as we may perpetuate yeast cells that are very good at reproducing at the expense of the cells, which make us alcohol. This would be a good baker's yeast but no good for brewing.

Furthermore, the foam at the top is most likely to contain wild yeasts and other bacteria, which are enemies of the wort.

No! We have to wait for the anaerobic phase. This is when the yeast is starved of oxygen, (having used all the dissolved oxygen in the wort and the atmospheric oxygen at the top of the fermentation vat) and is suffocated into working anaerobically. Only now is it producing mainly alcohol.

But we don't want the sediment at the bottom either as this is rich in all sorts of substances, which have precipitated out the wort and may have nothing to do with yeast. It will also contain dead yeast cells and others, which for one reason or another didn't find the wort to their liking. And an early sinker is not going to make a good top fermenting yeast, which is what the house-brewer is using much of the time.

It's not such a good idea to use the lees from a keg either, as the beer at the end of a five-gallon brew is probably well past its best and may already have been contaminated with air from the day the beer was syphoned into the keg. Talking of beer being well past its best, do remember that beer, unlike wine, only improves with age until it is mature. It holds its peak for about 6 weeks and then begins to decline.

So what is there left after we have rejected the tops and bottoms? The best procedure is to chose a strong ale (SG greater than 1065) you've just brewed and is ready for kegging. Take a small glass screw top bottle and sterilize it and the lid in a pressure cooker or microwave. Fill the bottle to the top with the fermented out young beer and screw it down securely. Keep it just under the cooling coils at the top back of the fridge, where you should achieve temperatures around 4°C (39°F).

You can keep this sample around six to ten weeks, after which it should be discarded if it hasn't been used. Some brewers put a small amount of sodium metabisulphite to the sample to kill bacteria and prevent oxidation by any dissolved air in the beer. Sodium metabisulphite doesn't stop yeast in its tracks but surely must give it a hard time. A well-fermented wort will contain little air so this addition of chemicals shouldn't be necessary.

To use the sample, just open the bottle about 2 days before you need it and decant off most of the liquid. Add the solid residue to a sterile wort, fit a fermentation lock and leave warm (20°C, 68°F) for a few days until needed. Then look at it carefully and if things look good, add it to your new wort in the usual way.

Historically one had to propagate one's own yeast. There was no handy homebrew retailer at the end of the street with a sealed sachet to get you started again. If things went wrong for our old time brewer, and he lost his yeast strain, he would have to go cap in hand to a neighbouring brewer and beg some yeast from him. There were often laws obliging brewers to supply their competitors with yeast at a nominal charge and this was necessary to prevent breweries being put out of business. Furthermore, the brewery was expected to supply the local bakers with their excess yeast, for the bakery only used yeast. It didn't produce any. Up until the middle of the eighteenth century yeast was probably supplied as a sample of wort. There are many bread and cake recipes still around which include the use of beer and I suspect the public missed the flavour that the wort gave to a baking, and so would add beer as an extra when yeast was no longer supplied to the baker as wort.

It was never a happy practice to try and keep yeast in a wort medium. Keeping it long enough to supply a baker on a daily basis was no problem but until the beginning of the nineteenth century it was common to suspend brewing during the summer months *(cf. Porter)*. Presumably the brewer had to keep a selection of worts ready through the summer months and start them for use by bakers and distillers. It was not feasible to keep working worts that long, and the brewer had to take a working yeast and revive it with fresh sterile wort every few weeks. If he were not brewing during the summer months then he had to maintain a variety of sterile worts from his last winter brews as well. He also had to keep one wort back to restart his own first brew in autumn. The distribution of these worts to bakers and distillers was taken over by middle men and it was they who realised that they could reduce the bulk of the wort and their work load by settling the yeast out, discarding the liquid and then pressing as much moisture as possible from the residue. This active pressed yeast is still available today and for baking purposes it is considerably better than dried yeasts. So buying a yeast culture and then propagating it, is really the only historically accurate way to make a beer. Here is how to press a yeast.

Pressed yeasts.

1) Design your fermentation vessel so that the yeast slurry can be drawn off from the bottom. An idea for a suitable construction is given under *Brewhouse Suggestions.* *(Page 111)*
2) As the fermentation progresses a considerable amount of material coagulates and settles out. Take this off daily and discard. The healthy yeast is among the last things to sink right to the bottom, so wait until the beer begins to clear and collect this sediment having discarded everything prior.
3) The yeast slurry can be kept in a fridge and used when needed as it is. Settling the yeast residue out from a yeast slurry can be speeded up with a centrifuge. Decant off the liquid, tap the solid onto a fine woven flannel, press out any remaining liquid and wrap the yeast in cling film.

   (Centrifuges are not very expensive but be careful about using one obtained second hand especially if it has been in use in a medical laboratory. A good swabbing down with plenty of bleach would be the minimum requirement before use in the brewhouse. As we shall not have to face distribution problems, it may be appropriate to rely on liquid cultures unless you can be sure where the centrifuge came from).

Yeast prepared in this way will keep around 1 week in the fridge. If longer storage is needed then the addition of sodium metabisulphite to the slurry is recommended. Eighteenth century brewers obviously kept yeast anything up to six months by keeping enough worts back and propagating through the summer. This was certainly risky and not something I would advise we try to imitate, especially as modern microbiology can help us with liquid and slant cultures. These are expensive in liquid form but one can work just as well with slants.

Pilsner with a slant.

Here is a genuine recipe for Pilsner. I chose this type of beer as an example of good use of yeast cultures because these fine bottom fermented light beers are the most difficult to get right. I use this recipe regularly when my wife gets desperate for a bit of home and needs a Continental beer to make England seem right again. It should make 4 gallons of beer very similar to Becks, the famous North German Bremen Pilsner at around 4.5% alcohol from a SG of 1045.

Ingredients.

Pale Lager Malt	*3 kg.*
Acid Malt	*100g.*
Carapils Malt	*100g.*
Saaz or Hallertauer Hops (alpha-acid 2%)	*50g.*
Hallertauer Hops (alpha-acid 2%)	*25g (finishing).*
Water	*14 litres (3 gallons) soft or boiled for 1 hour if necessary.*

Brew Tek North German Lager mini slant CL-660.

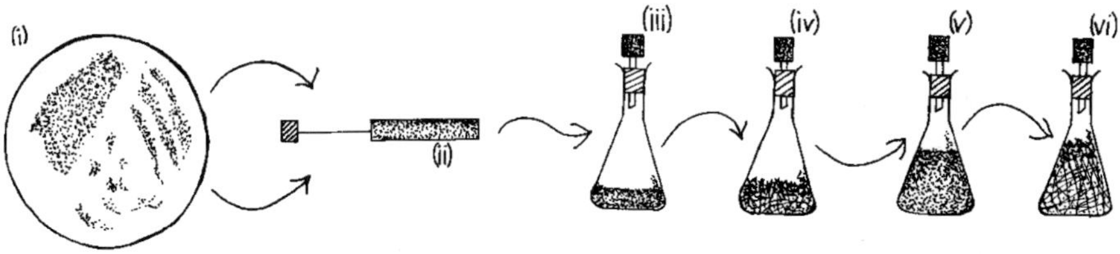

Yeast from a home made or commercially produced sample is started by choosing a single colony from the agar nutrient (i) and transferring it with the sterile loop (ii) to 50ml of sterile wort or starter (iii). The growing yeast is divided every 2-3 days into new sterile starters (iii), (iv), (v) and (vi) to produce four times the concentration of yeast starter.

Starting your yeast.

Brew Tek yeasts come in sealed pairs of Petri-dishes, called slants. They contain a yeast nutrient inoculated with yeast cells. You can store your slant in the fridge for anything up to a year, provided it is unopened and has been packed or used under sterile conditions. By the time they reach you they will be growing and beginning to colonise the nutrient. Dishes should be stored upside down, with the nutrient on top to prevent condensation dripping onto it. If you keep a slant that has been opened and it no longer looks like the unopened one supplied by Brew Tek, DON'T open it. Put it in a strong plastic bag, seal it and throw it away or incinerate it. Here is how to start your slant ready for pitching.

1) Set up a sterile environment by sanitizing your work area and hands with a common disinfectant. Work near a gas flame to provide a sterile air current.
2) Have a fresh piece of tape of the right length handy to reseal the dishes. Decide on a yeast colony you wish to transfer. The smaller the one you transfer, the purer it is likely to be. Open the dishes by peeling back the tape.
3) Sterilise the inoculating ring supplied, in the flame. Open the dishes just far enough to scoop out the colony you want and put it in a sterile bottle of Super Starter, seal and swirl. Close and reseal the Petri-dishes as soon as possible.
4) The next day take a sample of boiled Super Wort or a McCartney bottle of you own sterile wort. In the same sterile environment mix the starter and wort, fit with an air lock, swirl and keep at around 20°C (68°F) for a further 2 days.

You will then have ½ litre of starter and be pitching around ten times the quantity of yeast cells. The lag phase, (I) and reproduction phase (II) should be appreciably shortened. (page 125) This is good news when brewing lagers where the yeast will have to work at lower temperatures. Furthermore you should be using a very pure strain, which will help eliminate any unpleasant side tastes lager brewers so often complain of.

Decoction Mash for Pilsner.

1) *Mix the crushed malt with 4 litres of soft water at 40°C (104°F) to give a thick porridge at 35°C (95°F).*
2) *Mark the volume of the mash on the outside of the mash bucket with an indelible pen. Make another mark at ⅔ the volume.*

3) *Ladle ⅓ the mash into a saucepan of at least 3 litre capacity. Avoid using aluminium pots. Cover the main mash and keep it at 35°C (95°F).*
4) *Warm the saucepan slowly with lots of stirring until it is at 70°C (158°F). Add more water if you are worried it will burn.*
5) *When the temperature is approaching 70°C turn of the heat, insulate the pot and let it mash for 30 minutes.*
6) *Bring the saucepan contents quickly to boiling and mix it into the main mash in the bucket. Stir well and the temperature should settle out to around 50-55°C (122-131°F)*
7) *Ladle off ⅓ the mash into the saucepan and bring it slowly, over about 30 minutes, to the boil.*
8) *Mix the mashes, stir, and the temperature should reach 65°C (149°F). Maintain this temperature for 2 hours.*
9) *Remove ⅓ the mash again and bring it quickly to the boil. Mix the mashes and keep the temperature 75°C (167°F) for 15 minutes.*
10) *Sparge and work up the wort as normal to achieve a starting gravity of 1045.*
11) *Add a good working yeast at around 18°C (64°F) and as soon as the fermentation is underway, drop the temperature to 7-10°C (45-50°F). The gravity should drop to around 1.010 during the next 8-10 days.*

99% of Lagers that go wrong are because home brewers are notorious fiddlers. We probably wouldn't be home brewing if we weren't. But repeatedly taking the lid off to see how it is going is the kiss of death to a good Lager. Becks and Jever Pils *(two of the world's finest Pilsners)* are fermented in sterile rooms with access limited to the brewmaster and his personal assistant and they only go in if absolutely necessary, scrubbed up like a pair of brain surgeons. So that is the German way. Watch a Belgian fermentation and it wouldn't be obvious that it is the same process. If it is wild flavours that are to be eliminated, then copy the Germans.

12) *Keg the beer and store it at 8°C (46°F) or below.*

Many German brewers shock cool it to around 2°C (36°F) for a few days to help precipitate out any insoluble material.

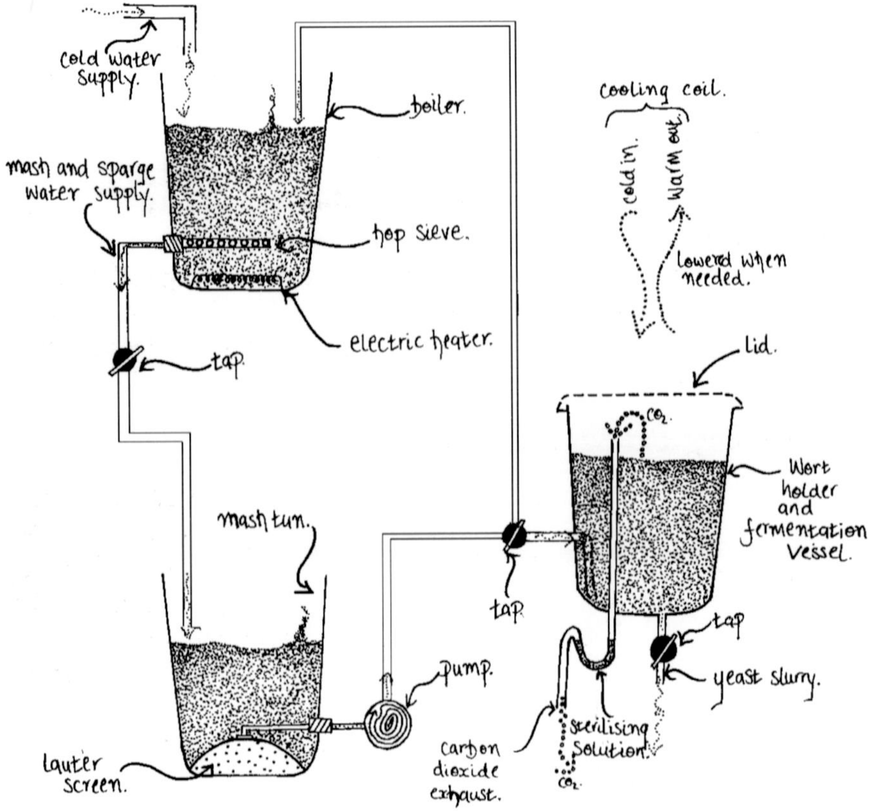

Rotating wort brew-system (after Loudon).

(i) Cold water is heated in the boiler and then gravity fed to the grain in the mash tun.
(ii) Once the mash becomes cold, the pump lifts the wort back to the heater to be warmed and then it is run back onto the draff.
(iii) When the mash is completed, the wort is pumped to the holding vessel. A rotating sparge arm is fitted to the mash tun. This is driven by the gravity fed water from the boiler.
(iv) Once sparging is completed, the combined wort and sparges are pumped to the boiler, brought to the boil and the hops added.
(v) The wort is now gravity fed to the fermentation vessel and a wort chiller lowered.
(vi) Yeast can be pitched and the carbon dioxide escapes through the U-tube. Yeast slurry and other solids can be drawn off and then the young beer gravity fed into kegs or bottles.

All vessels made from polypropylene. Pipework and unions from central heating PVC pipe.

Maturing.

It will take at least 8 weeks to mature at these temperatures and may taste medicinal after this time. Then give it another 4 weeks. And if it still isn't right then just keep on waiting!

Brew Tech claim 75% floculation and attenuation. I believe good floculation helps drag some of those awkward flavours out of suspension and traps them in the trub. The most common problem with Lager (assuming you haven't let wild yeasts or bacteria foul up the long slow fermentation), is that the hops take a long time to lose their sharp medicinal flavour. But it will come right! If it doesn't then change your yeast strain!

Step Mashing and Decoctions.

Traditionally many continental beers were brewed using the decoction method described in the Pilsner recipe, which involves starting a mash at around 35°C for around one hour and then drawing a third off, (mainly the liquid if possible), bringing this third to the boil and then rejoining to the main mash, whereupon, after stirring well, the mash temperature should approach 55°C. This temperature was held for about one hour, a third drawn off again, brought to the boil and stirred once again, into the main mash. The temperature this time reaches around 66°C.

This was always a tiresome procedure, adhered to be only because the continental barley types then employed were supposed to be very rich in proteins and this caused lautering problems. The protein rest at 35°C gave the enzymes chance to work on those nitrogenous molecules, and reduce them to more water soluble smaller molecules. The rest at 55°C gives the glutens chance to break down.

Farmers are now required to produce malting barleys of below 10% nitrogen content and if they err above 13% they are likely not to be able to sell their crop, or only for a much cheaper price.

Apparently we really don't need to carry out decoction mashes as present day malts made form low nitrogen barleys, won't need the protein rest at 35°C. If one does believe in sticking to recipes, which involve a decoction mash and one is using the mash equipment suggested, based on nineteenth century designs, it probably makes less work to go for step infusions instead of decoctions.

The liquid wort is being drawn off anyway in order to heat it and keep it at the required temperature. At some point one simply stops the pump, heats the reservoir of liquid in the boiler from the existing 35°C to the next required temperature (55°C) and then restart the pump.

I have already confessed to my flirtation with barley for malting from a local farmer who cannot often promise his nitrogen contents are below 13%, in fact he often has the maleur of knowing them to be higher than the accepted specification. I'm pleased to get his barley for next to nothing. A decoction mash is useful and once one has got the hang of them, they are not much more of a problem than an infusion mash. A step mash using the circulating wort principle is no more difficult than an infusion.

Brewery design and step mashing.

Here is a nineteenth century recipe for an ale which I believe gently raised the temperature and was really a step mash process.

Nottingham Ale.

This renowned liquor differs from other ales mainly in the mashing process.

1) *Soft water is run into the mash tub at 170°F onto the whole of the grist by degrees. Stir the whole time. The last amount of water provides cover for the whole contents.*
2) *Ladle water from the underback and run again and again through the grist for 12 hours at least or until you find that the sweet has been extracted from the grains.*
3) *The plan of enclosing the hops in a small bag can save trouble. The bag may be suspended and removed when convenient to prevent the hops burning to the sides and bottom of the copper. The hops in the bag must be added to until the appointed quantity has been consumed.*

   Much of the excellence of Nottingham ale is owing to the fine cellarage it is kept in. In many instances as many as 100 steps descended to arrive at the beer store.

This old recipe is quite without detail but the mash instructions can be interpreted as meaning that the mash temperature is raised in steps; "by degrees" is the phrase used. As the mash water reached the correct stike temperature, it was run in and the next batch put on to heat.

No information is given about quantities, although 8 lbs of hops to 16 bushels (128 gallons) of malt seems to be average. We don't know if the malt had already been crushed, but there are about 1.8 kg (4 lbs.) unbroken malt to the gallon. Water was added to render the required strength.

Another recipe from the same source *(The Art and Mystery of Brewing)* gets closer to the Hahn Brewing machine.

Scotch Ale.

Ingredients.

Pale malt	*8 bushels.*
Pale hops	*4 lbs.*
Water	*appropriate to required strength.*

Data. *Good bottling ale. Travels thousands of miles during which it increases in goodness.*

Mash 1) *Make a sparge of tin or sometimes plywood, perforated with many holes which let down the liquor into the mash tub in the form of heavy rain.*

2) *One mash only is generally made and that at 180°F which provides on its cooling and descent for the right temperature. After mashing 30 minutes, sometimes less and sometimes more, it is allowed to remain quiet for 3 hours and then run off. This sprinkling is done with 4 gallons of liquor and is repeated until the whole of thevirtue of the grist is extracted, each repetition remaining on the malt 30 minutes.*

The wort is poured similarly into the others and set to ferment at an unusually low temperature as low as 52°F. It will continue to work for two to three weeks, the bung lightly set in or the aperture covered only with a tile or a piece of slate and is not put in the cask until perfectly fine.

Honey is sometimes added if this appeals.

This mash is more like a non-stop fresh water sparge. Hahn and others recycled the wort.

Stubble Ale.

This beer was also designed for the rotating wort system, before house-brewers had the equipment to cycle the wort easily. It comes with the warning, "This is accounted a good form of liquor, but requires much diligence in brewing."

Method *When the water is ready, (boiling), throw in a couple of pails of cold water. Add the malt, about ½ bushel at a time. Stir well until all is absorbed, giving it a coating of malt or sweet bran.*

Keep hot for at least 3 hours. See then if the mash has sunk in the centre and in case it has, fill up with boiling water to a level with the edges of the mash.

Let stand ¾ hour and then run off the liquor in a reasonable stream which must be returned on the grains. Continually return a small pail full until you have extracted all the virtue from the grist.

Whenever the liquor is recommended to be returned on the grains it should be poured on as far from the tap as may be. Your worts will be procured much clearer. Let your mash stand 1 hour.

For this quantity 4 lbs of fine hops must be used by first rubbing and placing in a sieve for the wort to run on.

3½ bushels pale malt yield 1 barrel (36 gallons) of excellent ale.

Yet another method of flavouring the wort, this time by running the hot wort over the hops. This must have made a very aromatic beer with only very moderate bittering (cf. Oat Ale).

Sparging the wort.

Traditionally sparging involved slurrying the draff with new aliquots of hot water and then running these off. The modern brewery has for some time used the more efficient method of spraying the draff with hot water at around 70-75°C (158-167°F) and allowing the water to seep through the draff. House-brewers have always dreamed of imitating this most efficient method of washing the extract from the draff, often with quite abysmal results. The problem has always been to keep the water flow slow enough so as not to flood the draff, which results in the water running off the side or through a few channels it makes for itself and not percolating the draff at all. The whole situation becomes even more fraught if the malt has been ground instead of crushed, for then the draff floods and never drains even if left hours.

New design sparge arms are coming onto the market, which enable a very small spray of hot water to run down over the draff. They actually work on the same principle as a lawn sprinkler. The only difference is that the water is gravity fed at low pressure to the sparge arm and as it runs out through the tiny holes in the arms, it causes them to rotate, thereby giving an even distribution of water over the entire draff. Such sparge arms are fairly cheap to purchase and quite tedious to make. Certainly one could fabricate something sensible from micro-bore copper tubing but I doubt if it would be worth it. I find that the same efficiency of extraction can be achieved by using the batch washing method of yesteryear and certainly an efficiently constructed lauter screen as described makes this very easy to carry out.

Boiling Worts.

However one has sparged, the wort and the sparge water are collected and transferred to the boiler. Here they can be brought to the boil and the hops added. Remember to decide in advance the amount of bittering hops that are to be used and these should be added as soon as the wort has come to the boil. The full bittering due to alpha-acid isomerisation takes at least one hour to complete and toward the end of that time some aroma hops will need adding as the aromatic oils will have quite boiled out of the bittering hops due to steam distillation. The wort also needs to boil until the hot break has occurred. This is the point at which the suspended solids have been swirled around for so long that the collisions between the solids causes them to coagulate and become ever bigger. At some point, usually after at least one hour's boiling, the wort appears to achieve a shiny quality. The particles are then so large that when left to stand they will settle out. A sight-glass on the side of the boiler will not only allow one to measure accurately how much water is being heated during sparging and mashing, but it will also allow the character of the wort to be judged and the hot break easily recognised.

Assuming the aroma hops have been added, the wort needs cooling as quickly as possible, during which time the cold break occurs and even more suspended and dissolved solids precipitate out, leaving the wort clear and appetising. If a lauter screen has been used as suggested, astoundingly little material will precipitate out during the hot and cold break. Nevertheless it is still important to ensure these two breaks are comprehensively carried out.

Cooling worts.

To ensure the wort cools quickly, allow the boiled wort to gravity feed into your fermentation vat, which is fitted with a copper coil made of standard 8mm micro-bore plumber's copper tube. Cold water is allowed to flow through the tube and this will cool the wort. Traditionally a large surface area was also used to allow heat to escape. This would now be frowned upon due to the risk of airborne infection by wild yeasts or bacteria in the brew house, not to mention aerial oxidation of the wort, but if water is expensive where you live then consider circulating the cooling water through a large area pan to give it chance to cool. It has to be said that although we nowadays try to eliminate wort oxidation by keeping the hot wort away from the air, a traditional beer wort was certainly exposed to air for some time and at least until it was cold. This must have affected the nature of the beer, even though air is relatively insoluble in hot wort. This is definitely something for the purists to look into for despite its drawbacks, hot wort aeration seems to have been standard practice.

Once the wort has cooled to 20°C (68°F), take the specific gravity with a brewer's hydrometer and add water to achieve the desired value, bearing in mind the alcohol content you need. Pitch in the yeast that is to be used and cover the fermentation vat.

Pitching yeast.

House-brewers are used to covering the fermentation loosely to allow carbon dioxide gas to escape. There is nothing intrinsically wrong with this procedure. Professional breweries the world over have successfully used open fermentations for centuries and there seems to be very little real risk of infection from other sources provided standard kitchen hygiene and common sense are used, and a good fermenting yeast is pitched. However, as we are looking for more elegance in our set up, why not fabricate a fermentation vat which will allow sterile conditions, the carbon dioxide gas to escape and be collected for use to carbonate the beer, should you have a problem with forced carbonation. Most important is that this design facilitates running off the yeast sediment before casking. A normal 22 litre (5 gallon) polypropylene brewer's vat is fitted with a tap in the bottom to run off yeast. An air vent can be fitted in the top or a piece of pipe run from just below the lid of the vat down through the bottom and fitted with a U-trap to hold sterilising solution. The latter is actually unnecessary provided there are no large temperature changes in the fermentation room, for unless the dead volume above the beer expands and contracts, no microbes will find their way up the pipe. (cf. Pasteur's famous broth experiment).

Fermentation temperature.

Don't underestimate the huge volume changes the dead air above the fermentation undergoes, during even a small temperature swing. A few degrees can easily change much of the air above the fermenting wort and introduce bacteria.

It is important to avoid temperature changes within the fermenting wort. It is well established that yeast does not tolerate temperature change and large fluctuations can lead to the fermentation sticking.

Fermentation temperature can be difficult to control, especially in hot summer weather. Where I live, hot days, around 28°C (82°F) are often accompanied by night temperatures around 14°C (57°F). This is deadly for a fermentation. For this reason it is worth insulating the fermentation vat so that warming and cooling are slowed. It should be possible to steady temperature variations to within a few degrees over a 24 hour period, even if one is unable to actually dictate what that temperature is. If a wort cooler has been included in the original design, then the temperature of the fermentation can be controlled by passing cold water through the cooler. This is not a long term satisfactory solution as it wastes a lot of water and house-brewers, by their very nature are not wasteful people. In winter the matter is more easily resolved by placing the fermentation in such a cold place that some form of heating is required. A cheap heating belt is then all that is required for a top fermentation.

The moral of the story is that we should perhaps revert to the nineteenth century solution to the problem. Brew only between the months of October to March but realistically it is not always possible for us to do that, nor was it 150 years ago.

Kegging the Beer.

For years wood was the traditional material for keeping drinks such as wine or beer. The Pilsner Urquell Brewery in Pilsen still used oak fermenting vats until very recently and kegged their beer for secondary fermentation into oak. This was no easy piece of tradition to uphold for the vats needed regularly steam cleaning and relining with pitch, but there can be little doubt that the oak and pitch gave the beer its own special flavour, although no one could have said "It tastes of oak or pitch." Their Pilsner beer was the original light beer for soft water with Saaz hops, and it gave us the whole genus of beers of that character, which now go under the general name of "Pils". Urquell, Jever Pils and Becks Bier are without doubt one of the finest beers ever brewed, but unlike Jever and Becks, Urquell is now brewed under licence elsewhere in the world. These beers are so expensive to purchase that they rightly belong to the delicatessen of pale all malt beers. Time has however caught up with the Pilsner Urquell Brewery and they recently discarded their oak in favour of stainless steel. I'm sure they were forced into this decision by the old vats being simply beyond repair and the replacement cost prohibitive. For this reason we are unlikely to be able to cope with the problems of using wood for fermentation or storage of our beer. Stainless steel would be my first choice of material for all brewing equipment but is also very expensive, especially for pipe-work and connections. For secondary fermentation and dispensing however, I think it has become important. The traditional polythene kegs have served well for many years and still rightly have their price to recommend them. The biggest problem is that their forced carbonation system is not idiot proof and it is all too easy to over inject with gas, and in so doing freeze the pressure release safety valve. It is also easy to think one has screwed down the top securely, yet leave a tiny gap between the flange and the screw top through which air and beer attacking microbes can be drawn as the dead volume of air above the beer expands and contracts during the months of maturing. There are obvious merits in choosing a room with a stable temperature such as a cellar or even putting a small air-conditioning device in your brewery. Such devices are no longer expensive and plug into the mains. They will keep a small room of say 8m^2 (72 sq. ft) at a steady temperature of around 12°C at very little cost. Don't forget to plan in where you are going to get rid of your waste heat. It mustn't be in the room itself. That sounds obvious but it is all too easy to purchase a cold air blower and then realise the temperature isn't dropping. In fact you would actually warm the room as no cooler is 100% efficient. A small cooler mounted in the ceiling, drawing warm air from the room and recirculating it when cooled, but putting the waste heat into the roof void is ideal. Providing a cool room solves another obvious problem attached to using 22 litre (5 gallon) kegs. Few of us have a fridge with the capacity to take such kegs to cool them in summer. But even if you have your beer in a cool place, it doesn't solve the problem of serving it. After all, we want cool beer but don't want to be sitting in a cold place to drink it. Going to your brew-house or some separate room every time you want a drink can become a chore and here I have no recipe to rid you of that chore if you remain committed to polythene kegs. Stainless steel Cornelius kegs deliver the beer through a narrow bore length of plastic tubing. If, like me, your brewery is not immediately accessible, e.g. is in an outhouse, shed or cellar then the plastic pipes can be conveniently run through a roof void or ceiling or floor space and down into your kitchen.

A piece of conduit such as electricians use, or insulated plastic or foam pipe, which is cheaply available from a plumber's merchant, will help keep the beer cool on its way from your temperate brewery or store, into the kitchen or bar area of your house.

Clearing and lagering (German: lagern - to store).

Another commonly observed feature of plastic kegs is their odd lautering characteristics. Every brewer who has used glass to store and serve beer knows that the beer clears in a glass bottle very much quicker than beer stored in plastic. There is no easy explanation for this fact but it has at least the empirical opinion of brewers everywhere. One reason may be that glass develops tiny scratches and these act as active sites and help precipitations take place. If a chemist is trying to recrystallise a chemical, he firstly cools the solution and then, if that doesn't help, reaches for a glass rod and vigorously scratches the glass beaker with the rod. Often, Hey Presto! The crystals begin to form. Why? Who knows? Surface chemistry is a complex terrain that need not bother brewers. Plastic however, does not seem to form these active sites and therefore the tiny particles stay in solution. And there is another argument for the active site theory. Explosives are often synthesised in stainless steel vessels because stainless steel does not form such active sites, (scratched glass may cause premature explosions during synthesis because of these active sites) and beer clears as quickly in steel as in polythene but much slower than in glass. This is not a theory I favour though, as it does not explain all the observable facts. For instance, the particles which cloud beer are not in solution, but are tiny colloidal or suspended particles, which for whatever reason do not settle out in plastic but are quick to deposit in glass.

Let's disregard the active site theory for a while. I favour the notion that the polythene may hold electrostatic charge, especially in dry cool weather and passes on the effects of this charge to the suspended particles within the young beer. They will repel each other and this will hinder collisions between the particles and prevent their size increasing sufficiently to cause precipitation. If this hypothesis is correct then there is little we can do to counteract this effect apart from putting an earthing strap on a steel or polythene keg. This is a bit much trouble to go to, especially as it may make little difference. The only sensible step is to invest in a glass carboy and carry out most of the final maturation in the glass with an airlock. This will involve force carbonating the beer when it is finally transferred to the stainless steel or polythene keg. Forced carbonation seems to work well, although it does not have any historical pedigree and seems to have been rather looked down on.

Glass carboys are an additional expense and take up a lot of room. If price or space are of paramount importance then put up with good but cloudy beer or use finings.

There is little doubt that the rate of beer clearing can be enhanced by venting the polythene or stainless steel keg. Both types of vessels are capable of withstanding enormous pressure and the safety vents do not need to come into operation until the pressure has built up to around 50 psi (around 3 bar). This is about ten times the pressure one needs to dispense the beer and there is enough empirical evidence that a nearly flat beer clears much quicker than one at high pressure. Of course we would never dare to allow a glass bottle to get up to around 50 psi. Is this the deciding theory then on beer clearing? All the evidence seems to fit!

NOTES

Appendix 1.

Some Hops, which are now available to House-Brewers

Please note that the alpha-acid values given can only be approximate as they will vary from season to season, according to the weather and where they are grown.

Name	Alpha-acid %	Type	Origin	Uses/Problems
Pheonix Admiral	11 to 12%	Bittering	UK	New varieties, which have yet to perform
Pioneer	9 to 9.5	Bittering	UK	New dwarf variety with some aroma, suited to dark beers.
First Gold	5.5 to 6%	Aroma & bittering	UK	A fine all purpose hop. Excellent for the garden as it doesn't exceed 2m height.
Northern Brewer	5.5 to 6%	Bittering	Germany	Excellent bittering in strong ales and lagers. Only the imported variety is available.
Galena	9 to 10%	Bittering	USA	A Bullion replacement in traditional stouts and strong ales but it bitters more strongly than the original hops. Care!
Yeoman	6 to 8%	Bittering	UK	This hop doesn't harvest praise on its own. Blend with others in British beer.
Target	9.5 to 10%	Bittering	UK	Use this very popular and disease resistant hop carefully in hard water. This is the traditional Golding replacement.
Brewer's Gold	3.5 to 4%	Aroma & bittering	Germany	A very highly praised copper hop, which leaves no harshness.

Name	Alpha-acid %	Type	Origin	Uses/Problems
Omega	8 to 9%	Aroma & bittering	UK	This hop has become a rarity but is a good bittering hop for the coppper.
Northdown	7 to 8%	Aroma & bittering	UK	A replacement for the traditional UK Northern Brewer variety. Very good for Stouts.
Challenger	5.5 to 7%	Aroma & bittering	UK	A replacement for the over sensitive Golding, which can be used on its own as a copper hop.
Saaz	1.5 to 2%	Aroma	Bohemia	Classic Pilsener hop, which may be used in huge amounts for its unique aroma.
Perle	3.5 to 4%	Aroma	Germany	If you can afford it then use this beautiful hop in huge quantities for bittering lager beers.
Spalt	3 to 3.5%	Aroma	Germany	Nice aroma and bouquet.
Tettnang	3 to 4%	Aroma	Germany	One of the finest all purpose hops. Beware of non-German imitations.
Hallertauer	1 to 1.5%	Aroma	Germany	A classic aroma hop finding uses in all types of beer. Can be used in large amounts for bittering.
Styrian	3.5 to 4.5%	Aroma Goldings	Slov-enia	Actually a Yugoslavian Fuggle with enough bittering for lagers and ales.
Cascade	4.5 to 6%	Aroma & bittering	USA	Classic US hop for Pale Ales and Bitters with lots of aroma.

Name	Alpha-acid %	Type	Origin	Uses/Problems
Liberty	3 to 4%	Aroma	USA	Use lots of this hop in all types of ale without risking harshness.
Goldings	3.5 to 4.5%	Aroma	UK	Becoming rare due to lack of disease resistance, but the traditional mainstay of English bitters.
Mount Hood	3.5 to 4.5%	Aroma	USA	Hallertauer derivative with good aroma and bittering suited to hard water.
Willamette	3 to 4.5%	Aroma	USA	Fuggles derivative with only moderate bittering power.
W.G.V	4.5 to 5%	Aroma	UK	A slightly more powerful Golding variety, blended for use in bitters and pale ales.
Bramling Cross	5 to 6%	Aroma & bittering	UK	Another Golding derivative, which can replace the lost bitterness of Fuggles.
Progress	5 to 6%	Aroma & bittering	UK	Good flavour, aroma and alpha-acid content.
Fuggles	2.8 to 3.8%	Aroma	UK USA	Fuggles used to be considered a bittering hop but breeding has reduced this. Used to be used in bitters, now really only for dark English beers.
Chinook Nugget	12 to 13% 13 to 14%	Bittering	USA	High alpha hops. Take care!
Centennial	7 to 8%	Bittering	USA	High aroma, high alpha-acid hop.

Product information supplied by Brupacks

Appendix 2.

Some currently available malts.

The drying, kilning and roasting temperatures are for modern produced malts and differs from the traditional malts used in historical beers.

Name	Origin	Drying Temp.	Kilning Temp.	Roast Temp.	EBU colour	Max Mash %	Comments
Pilsner	Germany Bohemia	35°C	50-67°C	80°C	2.5	100	May be used on its own in soft water or in combination with darker malts.
Lager Malt	UK	35°C	55-85°C		3	100	British version of Pilsner malt.
Pale Malt	UK	35°C	95-105°C		5	100	Basis of UK ales and bitters and used in Belgium.
Mild Ale Malt	UK	35°C	100-110°C		6	100	Essentially a pale malt with hotter kilning. Produces more non-fermentable material to give a round sweet flavour.
Vienna Malt	Austria	40°C	105°C		6-8	100	Basis of Märzen and Oktoberfest beers. Used to be lighter kilned at 80°C.
Rauchmalz	Bavaria	40°C	105°C		8-12	100	Basis of Rauchbier with the flavour of the kilning wood. May be a substitute for brown malt.
Munich Light	Bavaria	40°C	100°C		13-15	80	Rich light Munich beers are made from this. Used to be even lighter kilned (95°C).

Name	Origin	Drying Temp.	Kilning Temp.	Roast Temp.	EBU colour	Max Mash %	Comments
Munich Dark	Bavaria	40°C	118°C		20-25	85	Munich Dunkelbier malt.
Amber Malt	UK	40°C	95°C	140°C	90-110	20	Used for dark ales and porter. Little fermentable extract is available as it is kilned while still damp.
Crystal Malt Caramalt	UK	65°C			80-140 23-28	20	Essentially the same malts but crystal malt is heated longer. The high drying temperature means a glassy low extract malt used to flavour and colour bitters.
Brown Malt	UK	40°C	95°C	140°C	120-150	10	Nowadays not kilned over smoke and has merely become darker amber malt.
Chocolate	UK	40°C		160°C	800	5	Produces the rich flavour desired in brown ales and porters.
Caramalt Carahell Carapils	Germany	65-80°C	130°C 120°C 110°C		800 20-30 3-5	5 40 10	Dried very hot and then kilned to varying degrees to produce typical glassiness. They all improve colouring and head retention.
Black Malt	UK	35°C		160°C	1400	10	A pale malt roasted to just short of burning for colour and bitterness in sweet stouts and porters.
Product information supplied by Brupacks							

Bibliography.

Anon. *Art and Mystery of making British wines etc.* also *The Whole Art of Brewing*. Chapman & Hall. 1865.

Bickerdyke, J. *The Curiosities of Ale and Beer.* 1886.

Bogen, Hans Joachim, *Buch der Biotechnik.* Droemer Knauer. *Munich* 1976.

Burgess, A. H. *Hops. Botany, cultivation and utilisation.* Leonard Hill. London 1964.

Collected authors. *Hopfen, Malz und Wasser. Bierbraukunst in Ostwestfalen-Lippe.* Westfalen Verlag. Bielefeld 1994

Gerard, J. *The Herbal or Generall Historie of Plants.* 1597.

Hahn, J. G. *Die Hausbrauerei.* Erfurt. 1804.

Hind, L. *Brewing Science and Practice.* Vol. 1. 1953.

Hitchcock, E. *Kitchen Anthropology: Home Brewing an Ancient Beer.* Brewing Techniques. October 1994.

Huber, E. *Bier und Bierbereitung bei den Völkern der Urzeit.* Gesellschaft für die Geschichte und Bibliographie des Brauwesens. Berlin 1926.

La Pensée, Clive W. *The Historical Companion to House-Brewing.* Montag Publications. Beverley 1990.

Loudon, J. C. *An Encyclopedia of Cottage, Farm and Villa Architecture.* 1833.

Lutz, H. F. *Viticulture and Brewing in Ancient Orient.* Leipzig 1922

Mathias, P. *The Brewing Industry in England 1700-1830.* Cambridge 1959.

Müller, A. E. *Lehrbuch der Ober-und Untergährung des Bieres.* Viehweg & Sohn. Braunschweig 1845.

Parkes, B. *The Domestic Brewer.* London 1821

Richmond, I. A. *Roman Britain.* Penguin Books. 1963

Richardson, J. *The Philosophical Principles of the Science of Brewing.* London 1798.

Ruprecht, H. *Brauerei Haldengut.* Verein für Wirtschaftshistorische Studien. Meilen (Switzerland) 1993.

Stopes, S. *Malt and Malting.* F.W. Lyon. London 1885

Strong, S. *Romance of Brewing.* 1951

Index